ANGEL
INSPIRATIONS

ANGEL
INSPIRATIONS

ESSENTIAL WISDOM,

INSIGHT, AND GUIDANCE

DAVID ROSS

DUNCAN BAIRD PUBLISHERS

LONDON

Angel Inspirations
David Ross

For Isabel and Miranda

Distributed in the USA and Canada by
Sterling Publishing Co., Inc.
387 Park Avenue South, New York, NY 10016-8810

This edition first published in the UK and USA in 2005 by
Duncan Baird Publishers Ltd
Sixth Floor, Castle House
75–76 Wells Street, London W1T 3QH

Commissioning Editor: Naomi Waters
Project Editor: Rebecca Miles
Managing Designer: Dan Sturges
Designer: Gail Jones
Picture Researcher: Susannah Stone
Commissioned artworks: Becky Blair

Library of Congress Cataloging-in-Publication Data Available

ISBN-13: 978-1-84483-191-3   ISBN-10: 1-84483-191-4
10 9 8 7 6 5 4 3 2

Typeset in Perpetua and Poetica
Color reproduction by Scanhouse, Malaysia
Printed in China by Imago

For information about custom editions, special sales, premium
and corporate purchases, please contact Sterling Special Sales
Department at 800-805-5489 or specialsales@sterlingpub.com.

Note on abbreviations:
BCE (Before the Common Era) is the equivalent of BC.
CE (Common Era) is the equivalent of AD.

AGENTS OF THE SPIRIT

The human race has been aware of angels for as long as the records can say, and probably for longer. From the time that we first began to acquire a sense of the divine, help was necessary to bridge the gap between earth and heaven. As people came to worship a single god, this need became even greater. In the ancient pagan religions, local and lesser gods could mediate with their inscrutable superiors who remained in the upper heavens. For the followers of the One God, there were no lesser deities. But the will and the intention of the unseen, all-providing God could be communicated to humankind by messengers – created beings of spirit rather than flesh. These were the angels.

Humanity has always looked at angels with a mixture of awe, fear, puzzlement and envy. Awe, as accorded to a superior being, one that is closer to the divine than we are. Fear, of the unknowable, and also because angels have been the bringers of chastisement as well as blessings. Puzzlement, in that it is hard for us to define or envisage an angel: as hard perhaps as it would be for a creature that lives on the bottom of the sea to envisage the life of a bird. We can be sure that there are angelic

OPPOSITE: Fresco showing an angel musician (detail), by Melozzo da Forli (1438–94).

forms and purposes of which we know nothing, and which may have nothing at all to do with us. And envy, in that we aspire to the life that they already enjoy: we sense that the angels exist in a state of grace more complete than ours.

But, despite those feelings, we also preserve the knowledge that once, before time as we experience it, the unthinkable happened. A number of the angels fell catastrophically from grace, and remain fallen to this day, beyond any possibility of redemption that we can understand. But if divine grace is beyond their reach, we are not. They can influence us, and they remain a perpetual threat as agents of evil: and evil can often wear a fair face.

The earliest books of the Bible refer to angels, and they remain present until the final book of Revelation, with its prophecies of the Last Judgment and the end of the world, in which events the angels themselves play an important part. The Judaic and Islamic traditions are also richly endowed with angels, most of them shared with the Christian tradition. Indeed, the Hebrew Apocrypha and, later, the Kabbalah are valuable sources of information on the activities and names of angels. A phrase in the Talmud, that great compendium of traditional Jewish scholarship and commentary, tells us that every blade of grass has an angel above it, saying, "Grow!" In modern Jewish teaching, angels play a much smaller part in mediating between heaven and earth. The angels of Islam are more numerous than raindrops, and one beautiful saying in the Qur'an gives an angel to every raindrop that falls from the sky.

As the Christian Church on earth expanded and acquired a more complex structure, so efforts were made to parallel this with a heavenly hierarchy. Angels were classified by rank and function, and the nine orders of angels (see pp.44–5) became official Catholic doctrine. In the Middle Ages, some brilliant minds examined the nature of angels. In the increasingly materialistic and scientifically-minded centuries following the Renaissance in Europe, angels have not gone away. With greater knowledge of all the world beliefs, past and present, we know that "angels", or beings comparable to angels, are found in many traditions. But most people today would be less willing to accept the strict hierarchy of angels and be more inclined, perhaps, to view them as the ancient Israelites did, as transcendent beings – manifestations of God.

Finally, when considering angels, always remember this: they are the inhabitants of a spiritual region that exists almost entirely beyond our human horizons. They come within the range of our finer senses, our most extended apprehension, our most intense imaginative vision. If they came wholly within the scope of our understanding, they would be less than angels, or we would be more than human.

A CONSIDERATION OF ANGELS

"Angels are spirits, but it is not because they are spirits that they are angels. They become Angels when they are sent. For the name Angel refers to their office, not their nature. You ask the name of this nature, it is spirit; you ask its office, it is that of an Angel, which is a messenger."

ST AUGUSTINE (354–430CE)

St Augustine provides a succinct definition of angels (above), but there are many more questions about angels, some of which are anticipated below.

What is an angel, and what does "angel" mean?

An angel is a being of pure spirit, created by God, entirely free from matter or the physical world. The word comes from Ancient Greek *angelos*, meaning "messenger". *Angelos* was the translation of a Hebrew word *mal-ak*, also meaning messenger. So, as St Thomas Aquinas pointed out in his great theological work *Summa Theologiae* (1266–73), we define, and can only define, angels by what they do, and not by what they are.

What is the purpose of angels?

Angels are used by God to carry out the divine will, in great and small things alike. They are agents and messengers.

Do angels have bodies?

No, they are pure spirit. But either they can assume bodily form when sent on an earthly mission, or they can make us see them in such a form. An angel can take any form and may not look like our idea of a "celestial being", or a human being, at all. But angels do have the power to change things in the material world.

For the same reason, the question which has bothered many in the past, "Do the angels have gender, as we do?" is irrelevant. Angels are created directly by divine power. Humans are created indirectly by physical reproduction. An angel could assume the form and persona of a woman or a man. Christ said to the Sadducees that human spirits when they rise from the dead do not marry – "they are like the angels in heaven."

Why are angels so often portrayed winged and robed?

The inspiration of angels in art is to give the viewer a sense of their spiritual nature. They are dwellers above the sky: hence the wings, to show they are not earthbound like us. They are of exalted status, so wear splendid garments and are portrayed as beautiful, according to the artist's notion of beauty and the era in which the work was created.

Do angels grow older?

No, because they are bodiless spirits. But

angels are not immortal. Their lives have a term, unthinkably long to us perhaps, but appointed by the Creator.

What are cherubs?

It is a commonly held misconception that cherubs are chubby winged babes, as most popularly depicted in the art of the Renaissance. They are, in fact, the Cherubim, one of the nine orders of angels (see pp.44–5). These are lofty, brilliant, awe-inspiring, holy and terrible creatures, and their original Prince was he who now rules the other Fallen ones. The origins of the name go back to a word meaning "pray" or "bless" in the ancient Akkadian language of the Middle East.

The concept of the cherub as baby emerged in the art of the Renaissance because this was a time of rediscovery of the classical world, and Cupid, the winged infant god of love from Roman mythology, became a favourite subject of painters. But Cupid was too pagan a subject for some patrons so, increasingly, he lost his arrows and became a *putto* (Italian for "little boy") – a baby angel. There are many lovely and well-known images of *putti*. Along with this representation of adorable child-angels gradually grew a sentimental feeling that these angels protected children; or that children who died became little angels. But it must be said that the cherubs of the painters and sculptors, for all their charm and sentimental appeal, are little more than a wildly romanticized view of angels.

OPPOSITE: Ceiling painting, by Andrea Mantegna (*c.*1431–1506), in the Ducal Palace, Mantua.

What language do angels speak?

Joan of Arc spoke with angels in medieval French; William Blake in 18th-century English. In modern times angels have appeared speaking many languages, according to the tongue of the person visited. But some witnesses, such as the 18th-century philosopher Emanuel Swedenborg and Rudolf Steiner in the early 20th century, have described angel speech as other than human. They split it into consonants, expressing ideas, and vowels, expressing affection. Steiner associated these respectively with the colours red and green, as if they vibrated within his mind rather than his eardrums. That is probably the key to angel speech: however it sounds or seems, it is a communication directly into our minds.

St Thomas Aquinas established that the angels speak among themselves in a way akin to telepathy.

How many angels are there?

The number of angels is uncountably vast. We perceive angels as intermediaries and as messengers to us. But to who else? Perhaps we are just one small component of the universe requiring angelic attention. And as angels were created to proclaim the glory of God, who is infinite and eternal, their numbers are as unimaginable as infinity.

How many angels can stand on the point of a needle?

This question was said to have formed the focal point of a supposed debate between

OPPOSITE: *Mystic Nativity* (detail), 1500, by Sandro Botticelli (1445–1510).

St Thomas Aquinas and Duns Scotus, two great medieval theologians who held divergent opinions on many points of Christian theology. In fact the two never met, and this hoary old joke question was never seriously discussed in the Middle Ages. However, it does relate to just what we mean by the angel as a pure spirit. Does it occupy space? If so, how much? On this point, as on so many others, Aquinas and Scotus disagree. Scotus is not always easy to follow, nor wholly consistent, but he believed, by intuition, that angels were composed of some sort of matter; whereas Aquinas, by reasoning, believed they were wholly spiritual.

Were angels created once and for all, or are new angels created?

This question is beyond our answering. In the New Testament, St Paul implies they were a single creation: "For by him all things were created: things in heaven and on earth, visible and invisible, whether thrones or powers or rulers or dominions." (COLOSSIANS 1.16)

Is there such a thing as a bad angel?

Yes. Though we normally reserve the word "angel" for those who are benevolent, we should not forget the Fallen angels, though generally we use other words for them, such as fiend, demon, devil or evil spirit.

Can angels be summoned?

Angels are emissaries, but of God, not humankind: we do not own them or hold any kind of power over them. In the Biblical and historical record, they appear

to humans at the direction of God.
They may anticipate, or respond to, our
distress, our needs, or simply our open-
mindedness. There is no evidence that we
can summon angels at our own will; and,
if we attempt to do so, the wrong sort of
angel may well respond.

Does everyone have a guardian angel?

This large question is dealt with in detail
elsewhere in this book (see Guardian
Angels, pp.74–81). But there can be no
doubt that, throughout the history of
humankind, angels have exercised a
protective and preserving influence over
us mortals, both morally and, in very
many cases, physically. We shall learn
about many such instances in the pages
that follow.

Part One

THE NATURE
of ANGELS

Many cultures and religions through history and around the world have left evidence of their belief in some form of supernatural being that we could describe as angelic.

We are going to explore the range of these historical beliefs and experiences, right up to the present day, sharing what many others, for thousands of years, have sensed, felt, seen and heard.

THE HERITAGE OF ANGELS

Many people think that the earliest references to angels come from the Hebrew Bible, but there are even earlier references to creatures that can be recognized as angelic beings or precursors thereof. Throughout our cultural history, elements from different belief systems have been intertwined in the development of our ideas about angels.

One of the oldest known sources of angel knowledge is a text from the ancient Sumerian civilization, dating from around 3000BCE, which refers to "messengers of the gods": beings that are neither gods nor humans. The extent to which this reference influenced angel history is unknown, but it is clear that some writers on angels, past and present, have drawn kinds of spirit or semi-spirit being from the various religions of the world into their work. However, the most coherent views of angels come from religions that hold to a belief in one supreme God. These angels can be good or wicked, but are not independent; they rely on a Creator for their existence, purpose and functions.

OPPOSITE: A detail from an Assyrian stone relief, dating from the ninth century BCE, showing a supernatural creature with wings carrying a deer and a branch.

Around 900BCE, the ancient civilization of Assyria placed carvings of winged creatures at their city gates to act as guardians, and depicted imposing winged men on wall panels. Some of the names and functions ascribed to fallen angels in the Judaeo-Christian tradition can be traced back to the gods of Assyria, Philistia and Moab, who were so vilified by the God of the Old Testament.

Zoroastrian precursors

In the Zoroastrian religion, established by the Persian prophet Zarathustra between 1000 and 600BCE, the beneficient deity Ahura Mazda commanded seven semi-independent spirits – the *amesha spentas* (bounteous immortals) – which originally emanated from him and represented different aspects of his nature. Below these mighty immortal spirits were the *yazatas* (adorable ones), half of whom looked after spirituality and morality on earth, while the other half oversaw material and natural phenomena. Finally, a third rank of angelic beings, named *fravashi* (guardian spirits), acted as personal guides to individual humans.

The angels of monotheism

Much of our knowledge of angels today comes from the world's three major monotheistic faiths: Judaism, Christianity and Islam. But within the texts and teachings surrounding these three, echoes of the earlier religions they replaced can be found. A late fifth-century Christian text, *On True Belief*, includes a collection of old pagan wisdom and oracular sayings that can be seen as presaging some

THE WINGED SPIRITS OF ANCIENT GREECE

The thinkers of Ancient Greece acquired many ideas from the Middle Eastern religions. Plato (427–347BCE) and other Greek philosophers envisaged angels as the intermediaries between gods and men, and discussed the concept of the winged spirit. Interestingly, some of the attributes of the Greek god Hermes (Roman name: Mercury), the winged messenger – notably his government of the sun – have also been ascribed to the Judaeo-Christian Archangel Michael.

Christian belief. One such saying, from Apollo's Oracle at Claros in Greece, describes three grades of angels beneath a (pagan) high god.

In the centuries after Christ, the richest sources of angel lore were the Gnostic thinkers and the Jewish mystics (the work of the latter reaching its peak in the medieval tradition of the Kabbalah).

Gnosticism was the pursuit of intuitive knowledge of various spiritual truths, as distinct from the public doctrine of Christianity or Judaism. The Gnostics' appetite for secret explanations of the invisible world led them to ascribe many specific activities to angels, and to name them – a practice the Church was to forbid in the 4th century.

ANGELS OF THE HEBREW BIBLE

*Almost from the first page the various tasks of angels are described in
the books of the Bible. Of the many and varying roles they play in the
Hebrew Bible (Old Testament), some universal themes emerge. These are
described here, illustrated by some of the Bible's most notable stories.*

With the story of Jacob comes one of the most celebrated of all angel dreams: "And he dreamed that there was a ladder set up on the earth, the top of it reaching to heaven and the angels of God were ascending and descending on it" (GENESIS 28.12). Jacob had other dreams of angels (GENESIS 31.11) but also at least one real encounter with angels as he travelled with his family to meet his brother Esau (GENESIS 32.1); and the night-long wrestling bout with an unnamed angel (GENESIS 32.24).

Jacob is one of our greatest witnesses to the influence and strength of angels. His ladder, with its angels descending and climbing again between heaven and earth, has been a sustaining vision through many centuries. It confirms the role of the angels as messengers, and as executors of the divine will, but it also graphically conveys the continuity of their service.

OPPOSITE: *Jacob's Ladder*, c.1490, by an artist from the Avignon school.

Behind the recorded experience of direct angel encounters, the image tells us, there is a never-ending stream of divine energy reaching down from and returning to heaven, even if its purposes are largely obscure to human minds.

Angelic guidance

At the time of his encounter with the burning bush (see box, right), Moses was an obscure shepherd, with no followers and no gift of oratory. He scarcely believed his senses when the voice from the bush told him that his mission was to lead his enslaved people out of Egypt. "Who am I that I should go to Pharaoh?" he asked, weighed down by his own weaknesses in the face of a daunting task. "I will be with you," said the voice. The inspiration of that vision never left him.

Of course, that was a solemn and epoch-making moment, but angelic guidance could also take more humble forms. When Balaam set off on the orders of his king, to curse the Israelites entering his land, his donkey turned three times off the road, seeing what he did not: an angel barring the way with a drawn sword. Balaam threatened to kill the beast, but the donkey astonished him by speaking: "Am I not your donkey, which you have ridden all your life to this day?" Then Balaam saw the angel and bowed down before it. Balaam went on his way, not to curse the incomers, but to bless them (NUMBERS 22. 21–35).

Elijah, fleeing his oppressors, had his strength and confidence restored by an

ANGEL OR GOD?

The sense of the angel as a physical embodiment of divine energy has its strongest realization in the story of Moses and his vision on Mount Horeb (Exodus 3). A bush was burning, but without being consumed, thus attracting Moses' attention. It is not wholly clear from the scripture whether the entity he encountered was an actual angel or a manifestation of God Himself, but on hearing the voice that spoke to him from the bush, Moses hid his face in reverence and fear.

"We have patrolled the earth, and lo, the whole earth remains at peace."

ZECHARIAH 1.11

angel (1 KINGS 19). His people had abandoned God, and wanted to kill him. Elijah's angel heralded the voice of God, and dispelled his despair and lethargy with specific orders for action.

Angelic protection

In the book of Daniel, angels intervene to save the lives of three men thrown into a blazing furnace at the order of King Nebuchadnezzar. Astounded onlookers see four men in the fire, one of them having "the appearance of a god" (DANIEL 3.25). Later, Daniel himself, thrown in a pit with lions, survives because an angel has sealed the lions' jaws (DANIEL 6.22).

Incidentally, it is in the accounts of Daniel's dreams that we find two of the rare instances of angels being named in the Bible. First Gabriel appears, to interpret two of the prophet's strange visions (DANIEL 8.16). Later, another angel tells Daniel about "the great prince, the protector of your people" – a reference to Archangel Michael (DANIEL 12.1).

The visions of Zechariah are rich in angels, and here their watchful role is spelled out, as those whom God has sent to patrol the world. Proclaimed at a time of unrest, there is comfort in their report, "We have patrolled the earth, and lo, the whole earth remains at peace."

NEW TESTAMENT ANGELS

*Angels play a significant if peripheral part in the life of Jesus,
primarily as bearers of messages, including that which, in the Christian
tradition, is the greatest news of all. They also provide strength and
support to Christ's followers in their mission to spread his message.*

The New Testament brings one of the best-known of all angel appearances, made familiar by the work of many great artists as well as by the Bible story itself – the Annunciation. Just prior to this event in Luke's gospel we are introduced to the angelic protagonist giving similar news elsewhere. "I am Gabriel. I stand in the presence of God," says the angel to Zechariah, telling the incredulous old man that he is to be the father of John the Baptist (LUKE 1.19). Gabriel receives a more appropriate reaction to his appearance before Mary, when he tells her that she will conceive the Son of God. As "the servant of the Lord" she accepts her part with grace, dignity and humility (LUKE 1.26–38).

The theme of the Annunciation has been an endless source of inspiration, not only to great artists, but to ordinary people. In its combination of the human

OPPOSITE: *The Annunciation* (detail), by Ferrari Gaudenzio (*d*.1546).

and the divine, and its exaltation of the role of a woman, this angel encounter has a quality possessed by no other.

Angels in the life of Christ

Luke also describes the angels of the Nativity (LUKE 2.9–13) – the messenger to the shepherds and then the whole heavenly throng, singing in glory. A highly significant reference to children in connection with angels is made by Jesus (MATTHEW 18.10) – "in heaven their angels continually see the face of my Father" – and in his sojourn in the wilderness, angels minister to him (MARK 1.13). In talking to Nathaniel, Jesus recalls the vision of Jacob, with angels ascending and descending (JOHN

1.51), and during the long night in the Garden of Gethsemane an angel comes to strengthen Jesus. After the Crucifixion, an angel rolls the stone away from Jesus' tomb, with a noise like an earthquake (MATTHEW 28.2), and when Mary Magdalene looks into the empty tomb, she sees two angels dressed in white (JOHN 20.12) who direct her to the risen Christ.

Angels and the apostles

In the adventurous and often danger-filled lives of the apostles, angels more than once gave direct aid. On one occasion, the apostles were all arrested and jailed, but an angel let them out, commanding them to go to the Temple

OPPOSITE: Fresco entitled *Noli Me Tangere* from the Life of Saint Mary Magdalene, attributed to Giotto (1267–1337), depicting Mary's encounter with the risen Christ.

and tell the people about Jesus Christ (ACTS 5.19). The Roman centurion Cornelius was told by an angel to send for the apostle Peter (ACTS 10.3–5). Soon afterwards, Peter, arrested by Herod, was freed by an angel (ACTS 12.7). In the

MONS MAGN' IGNE ARDENS
MISSUS EST IN MARE ET TERCIA
PARS NAVIUM INTERIIT.

"For he will command his angels concerning you to guard you in all your ways. On their hands they will bear you up, so that you will not dash your foot against a stone."

PSALM 91.11–12

midst of a terrible storm, the apostle Paul reassured fellow prisoners on a Roman ship that their lives would be spared: an angelic vision had promised him this (ACTS 27.23).

Angels at the end of time

The final book in the New Testament, the Book of Revelation is rich in references to angels, who are essential agents in its tremendous visions of the Apocalypse. Here, the angels' awesome power is emphasized, rather than their gentleness,

sweetness and protection. These fierce, vivid images may at first seem to contain little that is inspiring to us today. However, they serve as a reminder of how marvellous it is that beings capable of such mighty acts of power should care so much for us. These scenes throw into greater relief those other angelic characteristics, of tender care and solicitous love for humanity. Many testimonies exist to affirm that that loving care, the ministry of angels, will endure to the end of the world.

OPPOSITE: An 11th-century illuminated manuscript (detail) of an angel of the Apocalypse.

ISLAMIC ANGELS

In Islam the angels are uncountable, and their number is constantly being enlarged. It is a requirement of devout Muslims to believe in the angels, each one the direct creation of Allah.

In Islamic teaching, angels are present in every aspect of nature, although the Qur'an does not describe their appearance. The most important angels are the *hamalat al-'Arsh*, the four throne-bearers of Allah; next come the *karibuyin*, who constantly sing His praise. These angels remain in the heavenly realm but others attend on earth. Here, the four archangels are supreme. They are Jibril (Gabriel), who inspired Muhammad and dictated to him the Qur'an; Mikhail (Michael), the provider, who brings comfort and ease to the faithful; Israfil (Raphael), who will sound the trumpet at the Last Judgment; and Azrail, who receives the souls of the dead. Beneath the archangels innumerable ordinary angels watch over all creation. Each human is attended by four angels, two by day and two by night, recording the good and bad deeds they perform in their lives.

OPPOSITE: *The Archangel Jibril Reveals the Qur'an to Muhammad During a Battle*, 18th century, artist unknown.

ANGELS OF THE KABBALAH

The Jewish mystical tradition of Kabbalah is a rich source of angel lore, with angels and archangels playing a pivotal role in the Kabbalist's spiritual quest to understand and experience, as directly as possible, the true nature of God.

The origins of Kabbalah lie with the mystical visions of early Jewish prophets, and the name comes from the Hebrew "to receive". Its teachings are based on the Kabbalistic texts, including the *Zohar* (Book of Brightness) and the *Sefer Yetzira* (Book of Creation), which date from as early as the second century CE. These texts tell us about the great angels Sandalphon and Metatron. Sandalphon guards the foot of the mystical Tree of Life, at the top of which is Metatron, the angel closest to God, with 72 wings and innumerable eyes. The Tree of Life has ten stations, the Sefirot, each of which represents an aspect of God and is overseen by an archangel. These archangels include the dazzlingly bejewelled Samma'el, as well as Raphael, Gabriel and Michael. In addition, Metatron and Sandalphon also stand watch over the highest and lowest Sefirah respectively. Each angel in existence belongs to one of the Sefirot.

THE HIERARCHY
OF ANGELS

*Many ancient sources and religious traditions take angels for granted
as an essential part of the cosmology of heaven and earth. It was the
Christian Church, however, that made the most concerted attempts to
define an angelic hierarchy.*

As the doctrines of Christianity were refined and elaborated, the nature and functions of angels were examined more closely. Christianity was advancing steadily, and its bishops were concerned to keep the faith unified and pure. In many minds, the angels were identified with some of the old, abandoned gods, and there was even a danger that angel worship might overshadow that of the Trinity. Unauthorized persons were liable to have, or claim to have, angelic visions, and thus to have acquired secret knowledge. With good intentions, the Church fathers wanted to put the angels in their place. To explain them was to prevent them from being idolized, and so to preserve true religion.

St Paul gave much thought to angels. He rejected the notion that they could intervene in the relationship between humankind and God (ROMANS 8.38). He mistrusted angelic visions and those who said they had them (COLOSSIANS 2.18). This scepticism foreshadows what would always be the official attitude to those who claimed special knowledge and insights. In his Letter to the Hebrews, Paul describes at length the superiority of the Son to the angels; in doing so his purpose was not to diminish the angels, but to extol Christ.

St Ambrose of Milan (*c.*340–397) was one of the first churchmen to set out a hierarchy of angels, but there were other attempts. Meanwhile, angels were being proclaimed and named in great numbers by all kinds of thinkers and

MAGICAL ANGELS

Parallel to orthodox teachings in Judaism, Christianity and Islam, and borrowing different aspects from all three faiths, there evolved a complex lore of angels with its own purpose. That purpose was to serve the requirements of magic. Self-styled magicians invented formulae to conjure spirits from the heights or depths. Priests, rabbis and imams deplored and cursed these conjurors, but in every age the heady mixture of spiritual yearning and shallow thinking has led people astray.

teachers. Many of them were on or beyond the fringes of orthodoxy – whether in the Gnostic tradition, or influenced by Jewish thought, or still clinging to elements of a variety of pre-Christian religions.

The search for a definitive guide to the angels continued throughout the first millennia CE, during which time Islam became established as the third major monotheistic religion alongside Judaism and Christianity. This clarity about angels finally came in the 1200s when the Church seized on the discovery of the teachings of Dionysius the Areopagite, thought to have been written in the first century CE by Dionysius, a follower of St Paul. Among these was by far the clearest statement on the nature and organization

of angels, *Celestial Hierarchies*. It is the source of the orthodox nine orders of angels (see pp.44–5). But to the embarrassment of later churchmen, Dionysius was proved, in the 15th century, not to be the author. The document was an ancient fake dating from the fifth century. However, the angelic hierarchy set out by "pseudo-Dionysius", which had already passed into the orthodox teaching of the Church, survived this blow.

The Angelic Doctor

The great angel student of the Middle Ages was St Thomas Aquinas (1225–74), known as "the Angelic Doctor", and one of the finest theologians who has ever lived. He accepted "pseudo-Dionysius",

OPPOSITE: Illustration of Dante's *Paradiso*, 1880, by Gustave Doré (1832–83).

"In the higher part of the universe a higher degree of perfection is found... "

ST THOMAS AQUINAS (1225–74)

while bringing his own blend of faith and intellectual analysis to the development of the concept of angels. He argued that each angel constitutes a separate species, and in *Summa Theologiae* he wrote: "In the higher part of the universe a higher degree of perfection is found, wherein one individual being ... is so perfect that it lacks none of the things that pertain to its own species, and hence also the whole matter of the species is contained within one individual being."

While many writers today continue to develop new "hierarchies" of angels, the nine orders of angels remain the most commonly accepted system.

The Nine Orders

The nine orders of angels comprise three "hierarchies" (also known as spheres or choirs), each containing three orders. The number of orders, nine, or a trinity of trinities, is significant. For the Greek mathematician Pythagoras (sixth century BCE), eight, or a full chord, represented man, so nine stood for a higher order of being. From the nine Greek muses to the nine worlds of Norse myth, the number is often found within legend and religion.

The First Choir of Angels

The first hierarchy is that closest to God and profoundly involved in the celebration of divinity, creation and universal continuity. It consists of the Seraphim, Cherubim and Thrones. The name Seraphim is associated with shining or blazing, an indication of their closeness to the Divine Source. The Cherubim play a role chiefly of prayer and blessing, and wisdom is one of their special attributes. The Thrones, akin to the wheeled chariots in Book 1 of Ezekiel, are the great supporters of the whole cosmos.

The Second Choir of Angels

The second hierarchy protects divine purpose. It comprises the Dominions, Virtues and Powers. The first order is the Dominions, also known as Dominations, who are defenders against evil. The Virtues' main attributes are healing and restoration; they transmit the power

to work miracles. The Powers strive against evil forces, like the Dominions, but also preside over birth and death, and are often associated with stars.

The Third Choir of Angels

The third hierarchy cares for all created beings, especially for humankind with its hazardous but glorious gift of free will. It consists of the Principalities, Archangels and Angels. The Principalities protect social structure and good organizations. The Archangels care for created beings. Confusingly, we also use the same word for the Seraphim, particularly those who are said to look upon the face of God. The Angels are the lowest order and have direct contact with humans. Caring for us is their main task.

REFORMATION ANGELS

Through the later Middle Ages, the influence of angels was on the wane. The misery and death caused by the Plague, which scythed through 14th-century Europe, undermined their reputation for guardianship. At the same time, the increasing number of canonized saints threatened to invade territory previously ascribed to angels.

By the end of the Middle Ages, the notion of angels was under threat. The Catholic Church had a greatly expanding army of saints, whose intercessory role in heaven could have been seen as making the angels' role redundant. This, coupled with the coming of the Protestant Reformation at the beginning of the 16th century, with its emphasis on the human individual's direct relationship with God, could have sidelined angels indefinitely. However, it did not. Although the angels play a more subdued role in Protestantism, support came from an unexpected quarter. Both Martin Luther and John Calvin, two key Reformation leaders, believed in angels and wrote about them, accepting both their spiritual nature and their multiple links with humankind.

"An angel is a spiritual creature created by God without a body for the service of Christendom and the church."

MARTIN LUTHER (1483–1546)

ABOVE: A 14th-century tapestry (detail) showing *The Seven Angels with Seven Plagues*.

ENLIGHTENMENT ANGELS

During the 18th century the angelic visions of a few deeply spiritual individuals stood out against the general mood of scepticism and rational thinking. Then, in the 19th century, as the pace of technological change accelerated, angels came into their own again in an undercurrent of Romanticism and spiritual experimentation.

New ideas in philosophy and science developed during the 18th century, when the Western world prided itself on its "enlightenment" from the mists of ignorance and superstition. It was not a good climate for angel visions. "Man is a machine," declared the French physician Julien Offray de la Mettrie in 1748. One brilliant short essay in Voltaire's *Philosophical Dictionary* (1764) ends on a mildly ironic note: "We don't know exactly where angels live: in the air, in space, on the planets – it was not God's will that we should be informed of this."

Angels were part of an older world of faith, vision and experience. In an age that felt that, as the poet Alexander Pope wrote, "the proper study of mankind is man", to proclaim a belief in angels was to be old-fashioned, innocent or eccentric. It took eccentrics of genius,

> *"Is man an ape or an angel? I, my lord,*
> *am on the side of the angels."*
>
> BENJAMIN DISRAELI (1804–81)

such as Emanuel Swedenborg and William Blake (see pp.67–9), to include angels quite naturally in their world view.

The resurgence of angels

But by the 19th century, angels were beginning to have some appeal again. Despite the vast increase in scientific knowledge and the rate of technological invention, many people were still uncomfortably aware that the oldest and most profound questions about the ultimate origin and meaning of the universe remained unanswered. There was a renewed interest in both organized and mystical religion. In dozens of hymns, sung in thousands of churches of all denominations, the work of angels was acknowledged and praised. And this enthusiasm was reflected in many and varied representations of angels in painting, poetry, literature and music.

Amid the controversy aroused by Charles Darwin's evolutionary theories, Benjamin Disraeli's famously answered his own question in a speech at the Oxford Diocesan Conference in 1864: "Is man an ape or an angel? I, my lord, am on the side of the angels," thus encapsulating that timeless need for a sense of the sublime in the face of material reality.

COSMIC ANGELS

In the 20th century, the crisis of spirituality that was threatened in the 19th century finally arrived. Official, organized religion has less and less relevance to the daily life of many Westerners today. But paradoxically, awareness of angels has rarely been greater.

Recent developments in cosmology – such as the idea of space and time forming a single continuum, or of multiple parallel universes in which our world could simply be the figment of the imagination of another, more "real" universe – render the idea of a disembodied intelligence less far-fetched.

Many who prefer to think of God as the Creative Source, rather than by any earth-given name, still believe in angels. This is based on the appreciation that we sometimes walk a narrow path between our own inner space and the external universe – two vastnesses that cry out to be filled. Swimming against a seemingly relentless tide of materialism, the New Age movement offers spiritual paths accessible to all. As we reach out toward the timeless and the divine, the strength of those invisible helping hands is of untold value. We need our angels still.

OPPOSITE: *The Village Madonna*, 1934–42, by Marc Chagall (1887–1985).

A NATURAL HISTORY

In their portrayal of angels, artists have drawn freely not only upon traditional sources but also upon their own fertile imaginations. In the representation of character, clothes, wings, haloes and angelic attributes there are often fascinating divergences between one artist and another.

The depiction of angels in art brings a compelling physicality to an elusive, otherworldly phenomenon. It is reasonable to guess that painters would have put great thought into exactly how they should go about representing angels, and no doubt patrons paid attention to this matter as well. Perhaps in some circles the conviction or virtuosity with which angels were shown was seen as a hallmark of artistic excellence.

Angelic character and clothes

Angels tend to have a youthful freshness to their skin tones, with generally rather benign, placid facial expressions, perhaps with a hint of a beatific smile. Usually barefoot or sandalled, they have their hair simply styled, sometimes tightly coiled. They are more often androgynous in appearance than recognizably male or female. When present as attendants to the Christ child, they tend to be portrayed as

OPPOSITE: Angels mosaic, 9th century CE, Church of Santa Maria in Domenica, Rome.

chubby babies – as if selected for their potential for infantile companionship. Baby angels in paintings should not necessarily be read as cherubim, however. In a secular or allegorical setting, they are likely to be *putti*, symbolizing profane love. When *putti* crop up in sacred art, as they often do,

ABOVE: Archangel Gabriel from *The Annunciation* (detail), 1440, by Fra Angelico (1400–1455).

they may still have an air of mischief about them, as if to suggest that there is no need for us to be entirely solemn even when we turn our hearts to religion.

In Renaissance paintings adult angels tend to wear Renaissance-style costume, either elegantly plain or richly sumptuous. They may have flowers in their hair, or a simple coronet.

Angel wings

The image of the angel as a two-winged figure is undoubtedly inspired by birds, as well as by the winged figure sculptures of ancient Greece. Angels differ from birds in that their wings are often raised, or semi-raised, even in the rest position. The arms, of course, make it necessary for the wing joints to be

positioned far back on the shoulders. Many artists depict the feathers with minute realism. Some angel wings have a brown mottling, which is almost certainly inspired by natural observation (Fra Angelico favours this style). Some depictions (for example, by Da Vinci) even show wing coverts – the smaller cluster of feathers that covers the joint where wing meets body. But angels in art seldom fly in a wholly bird-like way: they seem not to flap their wings, at least not below the level of their bodies.

In Annunciation scenes the raised wings of Gabriel in profile presenting himself (or sometimes herself) to the Virgin give the impression of a creature who has just landed, with an urgent message to convey.

MESSENGERS OF LIGHT

Stained glass in Christian architecture offered a superb way to reinforce the most important narratives of the scriptures and the messages they contained for believers.

Angels in a stained-glass window glow with radiance, as the sun passes through them into the church. The stained glass artists, and the patrons who commissioned them, were always deeply aware of the spiritual connotations of light. It is as if the glory of God were shining through the filter of our perceptions – or our belief – deep into our hearts. The angel is to the divine as a window is to light – a glorious admission of perfection.

Where taking a more subsidiary role in a composition, angels may simply hover, upright, like statues that have risen into the air, their wings symbolic of flight rather than being genuine instruments of flight. This treatment makes it easier for the artist to present a whole choir of angels as a unified element of the composition. However, the tendency in the age of Baroque and Mannerism – that is, the post-Renaissance period – was for the painter to rejoice in the variety of poses, costumes and instruments within an angelic choir, the compositional unity being provided by the massed circles of their haloes.

Artists who painted the Fall of the angels – that is, the nemesis of Lucifer and his rebel cohorts – had an irresistible opportunity to show them tumbling

down wings akimbo into the nether regions of the universe, creating a sense of chaotic apocalypse, while in contrast the ranks of angels remaining in heaven retain their formal orderliness.

Asymmetric wings at rest seem to be a common feature of late 19th-century Pre-Raphaelite painters such as Edward Burne-Jones who create a sense of drama in their dynamic compositions.

ABOVE: Angel heads on a fragment of an unidentified Tuscan fresco, c.1450.

Sometimes an angel's wings, instead of being vaguely brownish, are richly coloured like costume – especially when the angel is shown in its finery. Many artists of the Renaissance clearly enjoyed showing off their virtuosity on either coloured feathers or patterned costume. When both occur together we often have the strong sense of a real bravura performance being given with the paintbrush.

Peacock-tail motifs are occasionally shown in a picture: the "eyes" in peacock tails have the traditional symbolism of an all-seeing divinity, though there is also a more obvious reference to the peacock itself, another winged creature (though one with limited capacity for flight).

To dramatize the appearance of an angel in flight an artist may show the upperside of the wings as a different (usually darker) colour than the underside. This was probably inspired originally by observations of birds – shearwaters, for example, have this kind of patterning, showing an apparent change of hue from black to white and back again as they wheel over the sea first this way, then that, in large flocks. In the depiction of angels' wings, dark blue uppersides with white underneath are not uncommon, and sometimes the blue will shade into brown – another detail that is possibly based on bird studies, as in some species this is typical of the plumage of a juvenile bird.

OPPOSITE: Altarpiece detail, Church of San Domenico, Perugia, by Fra Angelico (1400–1455).

"Blake said aloud, 'Aye! Who can paint an angel?'
A Voice in the room said, 'Michelangelo could.'
Blake said, 'How do you know?' 'I sat for him,'
said the Voice. 'I am the Archangel Gabriel.'"

ALLAN CUNNINGHAM (1784–1842)

Angel haloes

The halo, like the wings, is another instantly recognizable feature of angels, denoting holiness. It is alternatively referred to as a nimbus or aureole. Intriguingly, haloes tend to divide into two separate kinds. First, there are those that form an unchanging circular background to the head, which doesn't move even when the head is turned to a profile view: in other words, the halo is presented to the viewer rather than being an intrinsic part of the angel's anatomy. The problem faced by artists who took this approach was that haloed figures with their backs to the viewer appear to have their vision blocked by their own haloes – as in Giotto's Last Supper, painted at the beginning of the 14th century. But in later paintings the halo is often attached to the back of the head as an angled disk, like a hat, and we see it differently (and usually in an approximate perspective) depending on which way the angel is looking.

OPPOSITE: *An Angel Playing a Flageolet* (detail) by Edward Burne-Jones (1833–98).

There are variations too in the size and importance of the halo. It can be quite skimpy, like a wisp of light, and indeed scarcely noticeable. Sometimes, though, it appears as a single or double transparent gold circlet either behind or above the head, owing its impact more to the intensity of the gold than to any formal qualities. Or it can be absent altogether. In some paintings, however, the angelic halo has a palpable solidity, like a gold medallion, and indeed it may have an embossed appearance, perhaps with a coin-like milled or studded edge. A holy text may be shown within the halo, and the gold may match gold trimmings at the hems of the costume.

A halo may also consist of radiant spokes of light, like a wheel without an external rim.

Angel attributes

Angels playing instruments offered more satisfying possibilities to painters than angels singing, and in any case open mouths were insufficiently evocative of heavenly music. Hence, the harp, lute, fiddle, flute, sackbut, even the portable organ, could all be deployed in the celestial orchestra. "Gloria in excelsis", ranged in Latin around the halo, underlined the musical message.

Certain angelic attributes are used symbolically as a key to identification. In Annunciation scenes the archangel Gabriel, for example, usually holds a lily because it is a traditional symbol of both his and the Virgin's purity.

St Michael is shown either in armour fighting a dragon (Satan); or alternatively holding scales to denote his role in the Last Judgment as weigher of dead souls. When Gabriel appears at the Last Judgment he is the trumpet blower sounding the "last trump".

The archangel Raphael is characterized by his pilgrim's garb of cloak, staff and pouch. He carries a fish – a reference to the sea monster he slays in the Book of Tobit.

Christian art may also show Jophiel, the angel charged with the eviction of Adam and Eve from the Garden of Eden (he carries a flaming sword); Chamuel, who strengthened Jesus in the Agony in the Garden (shown with staff and cup); or Zadkiel, who stopped Abraham from sacrificing his own son Isaac (with the sacrificial knife).

OPPOSITE: *The Annunciation* (detail) by Eustache Le Sueur (1616–55).

Part Two

COMMUNICATING *with* ANGELS

Personal encounters with angels have
been recorded from the earliest times
up to the present day. An angelic presence
may have appeared in bodily form, or as
a bright light, or simply as a sensation of
comforting warmth and love. This part
of the book highlights some significant
encounters between humans and angels
through the ages, discusses the role of
individual or "guardian" angels, and
offers advice on how to prepare for
your own angelic visitation.

CONVERSATIONS
WITH ANGELS

*Although the social and historical circumstances of angelic visionaries
differed widely, their common bond is the open-mindedness with which
they experienced the divine presence of an angel. Their example can
guide us in our own quest for an angelic encounter.*

In 1425, when Archangel Michael, with Saints Catherine and Margaret, visited the 13-year-old Joan of Arc in the garden of her home, at first she was afraid; then she accepted his presence quite naturally and talked to him as if he was a local villager. At her trial for witchcraft in 1431, she spoke of hearing a voice accompanied by a bright light. She said she knew it was St Michael, "by the angels' speech and tongue." The voice told her to rid France of the conquering English invaders. Later she led troops into battle and forced the English to end the siege of Orleans in 1429. Asked to describe in what guise, shape, size and dress St Michael had come to her, she answered, "He was in the guise of a most upright man," and would say no more.

The scientist and the angels

In the 18th century, Swedish scientist and philosopher Emanuel Swedenborg (1688–1772) found himself regularly conversing with angels, and eventually resigned his official posts to pursue his studies of the subject. He wrote that God had "opened the inner parts of my mind or spirit to be in the spiritual world with angels, and at the same time in the natural world with men, and this now for 27 years." As befitted a scientist, he recorded the natural history of angels in considerable detail, explaining, for example, how they breathe and speak.

According to Swedenborg we see angels either by their permission, when they choose to take a material form, or if our inner, spiritual eyes are opened.

ABOVE: Archangel Michael appearing to Joan of Arc, 19th-century engraving, artist unknown.

"...their bright wings bespangling the boughs like stars."

WILLIAM BLAKE (1757–1827)

"So great is the power of angels in the spiritual world," he wrote, "that, if I should make known all that I have witnessed in regard to it, it would exceed belief." His prolific writings, including *Heavenly Secrets* (1749) and *Heaven and Hell* (1758), influenced many and led to the founding of the New Jerusalem Church in London after his death.

The visionary artist

Swedenborg's findings attracted the English poet, artist and mystic William Blake (1757–1827). However, Blake thought Swedenborg rather too dry in his approach; in any case, he had for many years experienced his own visions of angels. As a child he saw a tree filled with angels in a London street, "their bright wings bespangling the boughs like stars."

Like others before him Blake, too, treated his angels and his experiences of them quite naturally, and it was they who gave him the inspiration for the texts and images of his prophetic books. This is how he recorded one particular visitation by the archangel Gabriel: "As I looked, the shape dilated more and more: he waved his hands; the roof of my study opened; he ascended into heaven; he stood in the sun, and, beckoning to me, moved the universe."

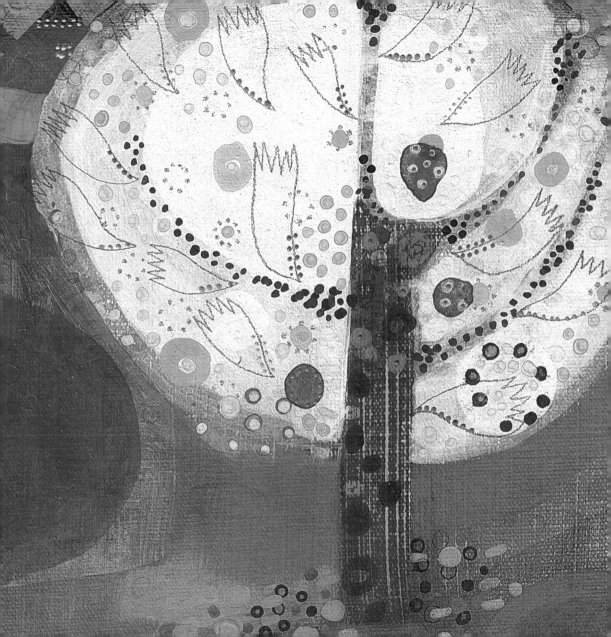

Blake's angelic experiences continued throughout his life, and when he died in 1827, he was happy and at peace, surrounded by the angels with whom he had lived and conversed, and who were, presumably, to lead him to the next world. These wonderful creatures inspired him to the end, as he summoned his last strength to break into joyful song.

Moroni's message

The meetings of Joseph Smith (1805–44), founder of Mormonism, with the angel Moroni between 1823 and 1827 were more like the visitations described in the Bible. Smith reported: "He called me by name, and said to me he was a messenger sent from the presence of God to me … that God had a work for me to do." Smith

THE BORROWED GUARDIAN

During the late 19th century, the French nun and mystic, Mother Agnès, sister of St Thérèse of Lisieux, had a great deal of contact with her own personal angel. It was recorded by one observer that "she made her angel do as she wished. She saw him, spoke familiarly with him, and I remember that, when I left her to go by dangerous roads at night, she gave him to me to help me get past the danger, and, when he had done so, he said goodbye to me and went back to the good soul he guarded."

"Who if I uttered a cry, would hear me among the ranks of angels? And if one of them were to clutch me to his heart, I would be consumed within his overwhelming being."

RAINER MARIA RILKE (1875–1926)

accepted his task as coming from God, and it is not recorded that he asked the angel any questions, although he did have other means of gleaning information about the invisible world. The angel told him of the location of a hidden sacred text, and two "seer stones" which would help him to translate it. Smith transcribed the text, with the help of the stones, into the *Book of Mormon* (1830), and this became the holy writ upon which the Mormons were to base their beliefs. Smith's angelic encounters, in common with all such visions which go beyond the framework of orthodox belief, were rejected by the established Church.

Steiner's hybrid vision

The Austrian educationalist and social philosopher, Rudolf Steiner (1861–1925), had angelic visions from his childhood, and elaborated his own system of angels from the information he received. It is a hybrid vision, incorporating elements from medieval traditions and Indian teaching, but a basic tenet is the notion of the guardian angel in childhood and later

A WALK IN THE FOREST

An eminent college professor, Dr Samuel Ralph Harlow (1885–1972), was walking with his wife one day in the woods near their Massachusetts home when they came upon a group of angels who passed over their heads. Later describing the encounter, Smith wrote of their amazement and exaltation at seeing a "floating group of glorious creatures that glowed with spiritual beauty ... six of them, young beautiful women dressed in flowing white garments and engaged in earnest conversation." The Harlows were too overwhelmed to accost the angels, who appeared to be indifferent to their presence.

life – a relationship which, Steiner believed, survives successive incarnations of the human soul. Steiner also described how to establish contact with the heavenly realms in his book, *Knowledge of the Higher World and Its Attainment* (1904).

Consumed by angels

Perhaps the most intriguing modern experiences are the unexpected and unsought ones. The Prague-born Austrian poet Rainer Maria Rilke (1875–1926), staying at the castle of Duino on the Adriatic, felt the place to be full of angels. They inspired him to write a magnificent sequence of poems, the *Duino Elegies*, but his experience was not – as is usually the case – one of serenity and peace. These angels were formidable, daunting presences.

GUARDIAN ANGELS

How comforting is the notion that each one of us is cared for by a personal angel, a being of profound love and power, in direct contact with God! This is one of humanity's most felicitous thoughts.

That each of us has a guardian angel is an assumption that according to some writers we are highly presumptuous to make. Others note that we only hear of guardian angels when some wonderful event has happened – an amazing cure or a rescue from disaster for which there is no obvious explanation. But what of the innumerable occasions when there is no cure, or disaster is not averted? As with so much angel lore, the idea of the guardian angel predates Christianity and is neither confirmed nor denied by Jesus' teaching.

Hundreds of modern stories tell of guardian angels – accounts of rescues, warnings, assistances. Angels are said to have averted car crashes, led families from burning houses, retrieved drifting boats. They have helped non-swimmers to swim in floodwater and have snatched children from the paths of speeding trucks. New stories are added every day. There are now numerous websites on the Internet dedicated to recording such accounts.

Angel rescues do not relate only to physical distress. Despair and listlessness

of spirit have also been lifted by angelic visitation or influence. But the majority of the stories do in fact tell of the figure who steps – or rushes – in to prevent a terrible accident from happening to someone, and then vanishes. Such extraordinary happenings are not only recorded by believers: many people with an angel story to tell begin their account with phrases like "I am no church-goer, but ..." or "It may seem crazy, but ..."

Individual guardians?

In the Hebrew Bible, Jacob on his deathbed makes reference to "the angel who has redeemed me from all harm" (GENESIS 48.16). But Henry Latham, author of The Risen Master (1901), and one of the most thoughtful writers on angels, believed that guardian angels were appointed only to children, and even then not on a one-to-one basis: instead certain angels were given this responsibility for all children. Adult humans, he felt, were moral creatures, meant to look after themselves. Latham also points out that there is no evidence in the Bible that angels can change or bend the laws of nature. However, the notion of the guardian angel is now so deeply lodged, and lent credence by so many accounts of personal experiences, that it cannot be easily dismissed.

Indeed, two early Christian churchmen firmly supported the idea of guardian angels. St John Chrysostom of Antioch (*c.*347–407), the great Bible commentator, thought their existence to be only natural: as he put it, "every man, it is true, has his angel." Gregory, Bishop of Pontus (*c.*220–*c.*272CE), who was born the son of poor, pagan parents, attributed his own highly successful career to the work of his guardian angel.

Angelic guardians in Islam

Islamic tradition assigns four guardian angels to each human soul, two to watch over it in daytime and two by night. These protectors are known as the *hafazah*, and their task is not to protect their ward's physical body against hazard or accident, but strictly to defend their soul against the temptations and attacks made by Satan and the demonic spirits, or *jinns*, under his control. Above all else, these forces of wickedness will employ all of their powers to tempt the believer to break one or more of the five basic rules, or "pillars", of Islam. Sunrise and sunset, the times when the *hafazah* change over, are especially dangerous moments.

But the *hafazah* also have another role, which is to record the actions of the person under their protection. They write down every single deed, good or bad, however trivial, committed by their human ward, and the record will be produced on the Day of Judgment, when the fate of each soul will be declared.

Eastern angels

The *devas* of Hinduism and Buddhism, celestial beings with control of natural forces such as wind, water and fire, have been likened to guardian angels, though they have many other tasks within the overall objective of ensuring *dharma*, the

Divine Law. They are less than divine, and like the *hafazah* they are in perpetual strife with malevolent spirits, the asuras, who seek to disrupt the proper order of creation. The *Rig Veda* describes their work: "May noble wisdom come to us from all sides, undeceived, unhindered, overflowing, so that the *devas* may always help us onward, unceasing in their care, our guardians day by day." Among the obligations with which the *devas* help are *yamas* (refrainings) and the *niyamas* (observances). The *yamas* include: not stealing; disciplining desire; abjuring lust and greed; curbing arrogance and anger; not lying; avoiding injustice; and shunning wrongdoing and evil company. The *niyamas* are: to be pure in body, mind and speech; to love mankind; to seek contentment;

to cultivate devotion; to develop forbearance; to give charitably; to study the scriptures; and to perform penance and sacrifice. Although the *boddhisatvas* of Buddhism have also sometimes been described as "Buddhist angels", this analogy is not altogether accurate, since the *boddhisatva*, though immensely enlightened, is human in origin, while angels and *devas* are wholly celestial.

Angelic presences

Many recorded appearances of angels in the scriptures describe no action, or none that relates directly to the mortals present: they are merely there – although there is also ample evidence in the New Testament

DIVINE COMFORTERS

Angels have often been seen around the time of a death, in the room where it has occurred, or where a body still lies. They are often described as "bright" and "tall" figures, but are not always winged. One account relates how a young nurse at a hospice saw an angel one evening – a tall, serene, shining form, radiating a sense of immense calm. It moved across a hall and vanished from her sight. In the room from which it had come, she learned afterwards, someone had just died. When she related what she had seen, her colleagues told her, to her great relief, that they too had seen, and felt soothed and comforted by the same figure.

of angels acting in a protective and sustaining capacity (see pp. 32–5); and there are many witnesses to such events.

Often angels have been seen in or near churches, but they have been seen in homes as well, like sentinels on guard. Some people have been escorted unawares by protective angels, invisible to themselves, but visible to, and deterring, those lying in wait to do them harm.

There are also numerous records of angels appearing to individuals, often in distress or need, because another person, maybe hundreds or even thousands of miles away, was praying for them.

At the doorway of life and death

In modern times many accounts of angelic visitations focus on the roles played by angels at times of death or near-death. Death is one fate that befalls us all, and it is also one of the most extreme events we can witness in others or experience ourselves. Little surprise, perhaps, that this is a time when there appears to be so much angelic activity. Many modern accounts of angels record their presence just before, during and after the moment of death. However, the presence of angels at this momentous time is in fact a time-honoured phenomenon. In the eighth century, the Life of St Cuthbert records how Cuthbert, while still a shepherd boy, had a vision of the death of St Aidan: "… through the opened heavens … he had seen angels ascending and descending, and in their hands was borne to heaven a holy soul, as if in a globe of fire."

ABOVE: A stained-glass window, by Edward Burne-Jones (1833–98).

OPENING UP TO THE ANGELS

*Experiencing an angelic encounter first-hand is a wonder that
is available to all of us. Here we offer suggestions on how to prepare
for an angel visitation, and give practical advice on how to
welcome your angel.*

Many people yearn for communication with angels without feeling that they are achieving this. Some achieve it without consciously desiring it. One thing is clear: angels, as spirits of good, cannot be summoned. Good angels, at least, are simply sent.

Some people's minds are relatively receptive to angels, possessing a natural openness that helps them to sense things beyond the physical plane. Others need to train themselves in order to perceive the hidden mysteries of the universe. The more we can simplify our complex selves, without becoming blindly credulous, the more receptive we can become. There is much that you can do to ensure that you are as open as possible to the presence and messages of angels. Indeed, there are as many ways of communicating with angels as there are angels themselves. Since angels are the messengers of God, it is He who chooses how they will appear to us or how we will hear them.

Finding your way

Today there is a real deluge of information about angels, including offers of guidance, and any number of definitions that link angels to days, hours, seasons, colours, auras and chakras, signs of the zodiac and other phenomena. How can we tell what to believe, and what to distrust, which method might work for us, and which won't?

The simple answer is by trial and error. It is important to remember that, while much of the "angelology" available today may have links with the theology of the main religions, it has essentially evolved outside the boundaries of the orthodox faiths. This places it in the context of what can broadly be termed the New Age movement, which allows the individual much greater freedom to pursue their own spiritual path, according to their particular needs, and to use whichever techniques of prayer, meditation or other ritual practices that work for them.

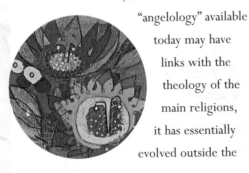

Trust your instincts

All of the new systems of angelic belief and practice will be valid for some people, but not all will be right for you. Follow your intuition, and maintain a sense of reverence in your spiritual quest. Angels are not good luck mascots, or fairy godmothers fulfilling our every wish. They are the agents of a great divine, creative power, and as such, you may wish to be wary of any practices that trivialize angels and what they do.

You will need to decide on how you wish to visualize your angel. Perhaps you prefer a literal, figurative image, such as those seen in Reniassance art. Or you may choose the more abstract notion of the angel as pure divinity, made palpable to an open intuitive mind. However, it is important that you do not become too attached to your visualization, because if the angelic encounter takes place, it may surprise you by taking a completely different form.

Initial preparations

The experiences of countless thousands of people through the years suggest some broad basic principles on which to start your angelic journey.

In order to develop the necessary level of mental and spiritual receptivity, you may first like to prepare the room in which you wish to receive your angel, to make it clean and tidy, perhaps to arrange some flowers, or to light a scented candle. These are good preparations to make, not so much because an angel will notice them or be attracted by them, but because they create a small external ritual which will help to prepare your inner self. If you wish to place particular objects of meaning in the room, remember that they are for you, not for the angel. You cannot lure or trap an angel. Clearing the barriers within your own mind is far more important than creating any artificial enticement.

OVERCOMING OBSTACLES

While each person will have their own individual psychological and spiritual disposition, it is possible to identify six common mental hurdles to overcome when preparing yourself for an angel visitation. Daunting as they may seem, if you deal with them one by one, using the suggestions below, they will melt away with surprising speed. The hurdles are disbelief, expectation, urgency, negative thoughts, pain and control.

✳ DISPEL DISBELIEF

"Why am I doing this?" "Can it be real?" "Are there really angels out there?" We live in a highly sceptical age, and thoughts like this can arise easily. They need not disturb you for long, provided that you are sincere in your search. This is not a modern problem — in the fourth century, St Augustine, struggling with scepticism, wrote this prayer: "Lord, I believe. Help thou my unbelief."

Think of your sincere quest — to receive an angel — as something solid and immovable, like a boulder. Then the doubting thoughts become no more than insects that buzz harmlessly around it.

✳ DISCOURAGE EXPECTATION

You may want the angel to come, very badly. You may want something specific from the angel. Put these thoughts as far to the back of your mind as you can. Your demand may be answered, or it may not. If it is, it's likely to be in a way that you could never have foreseen. Angels are not at our beck and call. Even if they give you something unexpected, it is

bound to be good for you because it comes from the Divine Source.

✴ BE PATIENT

Time means much more to us than it does to angels. Try to place your sense of time in line with that of beings who live outside it, or try to let go of time altogether. Don't have a clock or watch in the room. Give yourself an ample amount of time for your encounter, with no pre-set duration. Patience in the longer term will also probably be required since you may not feel the presence of your angel at the first attempt. Do not be discouraged, but continue to open your heart and mind to your angel, by

going through the preparatory stages (in pp.87–92), thus expanding your receptivity a little more each time.

✴ RID YOURSELF OF NEGATIVE THOUGHTS

As humans, we suffer anger, selfishness, jealousy, envy, greed, fatigue, and so on. There are many ugly instruments with which we can beat ourselves. Try to visualize these things as objects that you can physically lay aside, and allow your own spirit, which is essentially innocent and pure, to expand into the space left behind. This is the real you — the person your angel wants to meet.

✳ LET GO OF PAIN

If you are experiencing pain, whether physical or emotional, it tends to dominate the conscious mind. And it is often in times of hurt or suffering that we need our angels most. Make it possible for the angel to come past your pain, by visualizing the opening of a way in your mind to an area of peace beyond your immediate feelings.

✳ RELINQUISH CONTROL

By dealing with the first five hurdles, you have come a long way toward handling the sixth. You have already made room for the angel in your heart and mind. Now, finally, try to dismantle the rational boundaries that you may still half-unconsciously have in position. It's not so much a question of opening the gate, as of removing the walls. This is always disconcerting, as we are so accustomed to fitting our experiences to a familiar set of ideas. At first, you might feel quite vulnerable, but the result of relaxing control is not mental chaos. Rather, a new focus comes, and a new clarity: inspiration. Like many words normally taken for granted, "inspiration" is a beautiful metaphor. It means a "breathing in". Whether we breathe in the inspiration ourselves, or it is poured into us from an external angelic source, hardly matters.

Welcoming your angel

With the mental hurdles cleared and
negative thoughts disposed of, we can
turn back to the positive aspects of
preparing for your angelic encounter.
We've already established that your own
receptivity is essential. This doesn't
necessarily mean you have to feel totally
relaxed or peaceful. When we are in any
distress, it's extremely hard to achieve
this. But it would not be helpful to let
yourself become very keyed-up and
tense. Maybe the best analogy is to
suppose that a much loved but rarely
seen friend has said that he or she will be
coming to see you today. How would you
prepare yourself and your room for such
a visitor? Nothing different is required for
an angel visitation – a sense of positive
and pleasant anticipation. Be careful,

however, that this does not translate into
specific demands or expectations of what
you want to gain from the encounter
(see p.87).

Not only do you need to have a
welcoming state of mind toward the
angels themselves, but also toward any
guidance they may have for you. Because
you are trying to engage with another
being, you are opening yourself up to
receive messages or inspiration from
them. Since their messages emanate from
the Divine Source, we cannot possibly
predict what form this may take, or
what it may contain. We are bound
to be surprised, perhaps sometimes
disappointed by what the angels convey
to us, since the answers we receive to
our questions may not aways be what we
want to hear.

Final preparations

Some form of spiritual exercise completes your preparation. This serves as a final aid to calm the mind, and places your practice in a spiritual context. A short prayer, perhaps spoken aloud, is a good way of doing this. You can use the prayer below, or you can write your own.

After, or instead of, saying a prayer, a moment of quiet meditation is advised. We offer you a simple meditation to follow on the next page, although if you already meditate, you may prefer to adapt your existing technique. This meditation can become central to your angel encounters (see p.93).

A PREPARATORY PRAYER

Dear Lord,

As one of those whom you have brought into the earthly world, I ask for your help in my own small aims and purposes, within your great universal plan. I know that your angels are constantly about me, and I ask you to grant me the ability to sense their presence and to let your angels help me resolve my difficulties and problems.

All in your Holy Name.

A SHORT PREPARATORY MEDITATION

1 *In the peaceful setting you have prepared (see p.85), sit in a comfortable chair, with your feet flat on the ground and your hands resting loosely on your lap.*

2 *Close your eyes, and breathe slowly and deeply, drawing each breath in and down toward your diaphragm. Exhale slowly, and with each breath feel yourself becoming more relaxed.*

3 *Starting with your head, focus your attention on each part of your body, releasing any tension or stiffness held in your muscles and joints. Continue to breathe slowly and deeply as you do this. Work down through your head, neck, shoulders, arms, hands, chest, abdomen, back, legs, feet and toes, releasing any tension as you go.*

4 *Now it is time to quieten your mind. You might like to focus on a mental image, maybe a candle, or an angel, all the while still breathing slowly and deeply. Let any distracting thoughts flow through your mind, then calmly return to your point of focus.*

5 *You are now ready for the angelic component of your meditation (see Developing your practice, opposite). It is at this stage that you can invite your guardian angel to draw near, ask a direct question, or express some intention with which you would like angelic assistance.*

6 *When you sense that your meditation is over, remember to thank your angel or angels for their participation and any guidance they have offered you.*

Developing your practice

At step five in the meditation opposite, there are several possible ways to proceed. Perhaps you want to continue emptying your mind, creating the awareness suitable for receiving angelic guidance: simply send out an open mental invitation for your guardian angel to come to you.

Alternatively, you may have a specific dilemma or problem with which you need help. In this case, you can ask your guardian angel to help you find a solution.

A third possibility is that you may wish to develop within yourself one of the 25 angelic qualities identified in the next part of the book – love or compassion, for example. To incorporate this element into the preparatory meditation opposite you can adopt or adapt some of the practical suggestions found in the treatment of the angelic qualities in Part Three (pp.94–145).

Whichever way you proceed, express yourself clearly and sincerely. For example, "Guardian angel, please help me feel your presence," or "please help me develop more compassion toward my mother/brother and so on." You do not have to speak out loud, though it may reinforce your request if you do.

Interpreting your angels

The form and content of angelic guidance may often surprise us. Sometimes, it may appear too obscure or enigmatic to understand. Accept the first words or pictures that come to you, and keep them in mind until their significance dawns on you. You can always ask your angel later for clarification of their message.

Part Three

THE QUALITIES *of* ANGELS

While certain angels have become
identified with particular functions and
qualities, all angels reflect a range of
enduring attributes toward which we
aspire. The angelic qualities we sense
most clearly are those we possess only in
an imperfect or partial state. But each
one of us, wherever we are on our
individual spiritual paths, can be inspired
and helped by the example of angels.
In this part of the book, we describe 25
angelic qualities and encourage you to
develop each one in yourself.

HUMILITY

"All who exalt themselves will be humbled,
and all who humble themselves will be exalted."

MATTHEW 23.11

Although angels sometimes appear in visions of brilliant majesty, and are often depicted as such in works of art, their role is one of service – to act out the divine will of God and to care for humankind. In our competitive world, with its emphasis on proud display, humility might seem unfashionable, perhaps even a reflection of low self-esteem. But being humble is not the same as being submissive – it is to act selflessly, to practise acceptance of the universe and its many challenges, and to cultivate a spirit of service toward all those around us.

To benefit from an angel's message, you need to be prepared to accept its content, however surprising. The supreme example of this is found in the angel Gabriel's message to the Virgin Mary, that she, among all women, was chosen to be the mother of the Messiah. She said simply in reply: "Behold the handmaiden of the Lord." The humble beauty of that gesture of total acceptance is an inspiration in itself. Meditate on Mary's reply and try to absorb something of its graciousness deep into your own spiritual being.

THE HUMBLE HEART

✴ *Make a virtue out of performing any humble tasks you are required to do. Take pleasure in their simplicity.*

✴ *Spend some time meditating on the privileged awareness that we have of angels — this is a wonderful heaven-sent gift. Be conscious of the infinite magnanimity of angels as you humbly invoke them, or one of them, to reveal themselves to you.*

✴ *To maintain yourself in a spirit of receptiveness to angels, be sure to guard against feelings of superiority over others. In the eyes of God we are all equal. Work at trying to see the common spiritual ground that each of us shares with everyone else, despite differences of race, religion, age or social circumstances.*

ABOVE: *Virgin and Child*, 15th century, school of Rogier van der Weyden.

SERENITY

"Nothing in all creation is so like God as stillness."

MEISTER ECKHART (*c.*1260–*c.*1327)

The face of an angel, in many of the great Christain paintings of the Renaissance, is an image of pure serenity. We have only to look upon such a face to feel that there is a place of tranquillity to which we may at least aspire, even if we may not wholly attain it. By meditating upon such a painting, or even simply gazing upon it with full attention, we may be able to lift ourselves above our troubles for a while. However, it is not necessary to use actual imagery in this way to gain peace from an angelic presence. Another approach is to access angelic serenity inwardly, in the depths of a quiet meditation. Think of the mind as an inner celestial region where angels dwell. Heaven, we might even say, is to be found within ourselves, an inner state rather than a cosmic region. By sitting quietly, venturing deep into our own minds, concentrating on divine energy and allowing all other thoughts to drift out of our consciousness, we create an inner space where angelic peace can settle. And having created such peace within ourselves, we can do our best to bring peace too to our loved ones and friends.

A MEDITATION ON THE SERENITY OF ANGELS

1 *Sit comfortably in a quiet place. Set up a candle on which to focus your mind in the first stage of your meditation. Try to position it so that the flame is not too far from eye-level. Make sure that the candle is well away from any fabrics in the room, and do not leave the flame unattended at any time.*

2 *Breathe slowly and deeply, so that your body begins to relax a little. One by one, let the tensions fall away from each of your limbs, then progress from your head down to each of your shoulders and then down your back, loosening all the muscular knots and tensions. Try to relax your mind similarly. Let go of your inner tensions. Now look toward the candle, watching its dancing flame with concentrated attention. Imagine*

the flame as a bonfire the angels have made of all your worldy obstructions – the tangle of negative emotions and worldly attachments that have sabotaged your peace.

3 *Close your eyes and visualize the candle flame in front of you. Imagine it as the radiantly peaceful heart of an angel, whose peace is pouring into your own heart from this heavenly source. Let this angelic upwelling of peace within yourself banish your cares. If, during your meditation, your mind returns to one of its worries, ask the angels for help with that situation.*

4 *After completing the meditation, gradually bring your attention back to your surroundings. Extinguish the candle.*

AFFIRMATION

"I believe in angels: angels in heaven, on earth, and in the midmost air
... guardian or tutelary angels steering our wayward course."

ROSE MACAULAY (1881–1958)

Angels are positive beings, and they can show us how to take a positive view of life. To benefit from this, you might choose to make affirmations – that is, positive statements of belief or intent made in an assertive frame of mind. The effect is rather like that of convincing yourself of the truth of an assertion; or sometimes it feels more like making a promise to yourself. Make an affirmation of your confidence in the angelic world, and repeat it from time to time so that it works on your unconscious mind. Such guarantees of sincerity can bring you into closer harmony with the angels.

AFFIRMING OUR BELIEF

✳ *Write your own angelic affirmation and say it aloud three times a day. Alternatively, you could use the quotation at the top of this page.*

Or try working with the following statement: "I believe in the positive and guiding power of angels and welcome this into my life."

OPPOSITE: Drawing of Raphael, 1842, by Jean Auguste Dominique Ingres (1780–1867).

CONFIDENCE

The guardian angels of life fly so high
as to be beyond our sight,
but they are always looking down upon us.

JOHANN PAUL RICHTER (1763–1825)

Somtimes it may almost feel to us that doubt is one of the regular attributes of being human; while at other times doubt seems like a snare that our own insecurities have foisted upon us. To transform doubt into confidence the angel offers us a reassuring image of decisiveness. Having no emotional distractions or uncertainties to contend with, an angel always acts firmly and with one hundred per cent concentration.

TRUST THE ANGELS

✴ *Say aloud the following affirmation each day to build your confidence:*
"I am a child of the universe. I belong here, and the angels support me and love me."

✴ *If your confidence is being undermined by a particular person or situation, invoke an angel to help sustain you. Ask Hadraniel or Verchiel to impart some of their assurance to you.*

OPPOSITE: *Warrior Angel*, 1348–54, by Ridolfo di Arpo Guariento (*c.*1310–*c.*1370).

PERCEPTION

"We not only live among men, but there are airy hosts, blessed spectators, sympathetic lookers-on, that see and know and appreciate our thoughts and feelings and actions."

HENRY WARD BEECHER (1813–87)

Angelic perception is to human perception as a microscope is to a magnifying glass – it belongs in a different sphere of experience. When angels visit us, they see through our many layers of disguise. We may fool other people, or even ourselves, but the angels at once apprehend our true nature, warts and all. Amazingly, they love us just the same. If ever we can harness the powers of angelic perception, we will see the holiness of ordinary things and the virtues of ordinary people.

THE WONDERFUL IN THE ORDINARY

✷ *Spend a day making every effort to be as observant as possible of your surroundings and the people you encounter, seeing the divine within every created thing.*

✷ *Challenge yourself to an observation test on your immediate surroundings. For example, can you remember which are the most beautiful trees or flower gardens in your local area? If* not, spend some time reacquainting yourself with them. Practising perception in this way heightens your appreciation of your environment — and your own inner feelings.

✳ Consider whether you tend to have negative perceptions of anything — perhaps a person or even a building — and make an effort to find something positive or pleasing in them instead. You may not radically alter your opinions of your chosen subject, but you will stretch your mental boundaries and feel invigorated by the exercise. Always try to keep your perceptions fresh, avoiding the deadening effect of habit.

WISDOM

*"I have given you words of vision and wisdom more secret than
hidden mysteries. Ponder them in the silence of your soul,
and then in freedom do your will."*

THE BHAGAVAD GITA (1ST–2ND CENTURY CE)

We cannot hope to fully understand the workings of divine providence, but neither can the angels themselves – they are not all-knowing. However, they are given much more wisdom than we possess, and through them we may be granted some revelations which, however small, will be of great value to us. While knowledge comes from study, wisdom comes from experience. It is often the product of a life in which good actions and thoughtful contemplation are balanced in equal measure.

THE ANGELIC PRISM

✳ *If you face a dilemma or a difficult decision of some kind, let your guardian angel be a guide to you. Like a prism through which you can focus light, pass your judgments or intentions through him to filter out distraction and misdirection, and gain clarity and insight.*

OPPOSITE: Dante with Beatrice in Paradise, from Dante's *Paradiso*, 15th century, artist unknown.

SERVICE

"Praise be to Allah, the creator of the heavens and earth,
who maketh the angels his messengers, and giveth them two,
three or four pairs of wings."

THE QUR'AN

That the angels exist to serve (both God and humankind) offers great comfort to us, not to mention a valuable pattern of behaviour. This is especially welcome as some people today view service as an anachronism – a throwback to the old days, with connotations of oppression or subordination. All too often in the modern world we are praised for putting ourselves first, as opposed to working for the benefit of others. Ideally we should aim to make some self-sacrifices for others without relinquishing the most cherished and valuable of our dreams. While it benefits nobody to allow other people to bully or manipulate us, the idea of giving respectful service to anyone who merits it – by their intentions, their achievements or their misfortunes – is supremely sound. It is good to earn spiritual credit by selflessness. The law of karma dictates that acts of loving service will bring similar blessings back to those who initiate them. The angels, too, will be thankful for your help in making their job just a little bit easier.

GIVING AND RECEIVING

✳ *Emulate the angels' loyal service to humankind by offering to serve any person or group who is in need. The sense of self-worth in your life will increase — a pleasant side-effect to the help you will be giving.*

✳ *If your life already involves a large degree of service (perhaps as a parent, or as a worker in the care or service sectors of society), this can sometimes lead to feelings of under-appreciation. Take some time to consider the lives you have touched, thank the angels for their continued support in your own life, and ask that they enable you to continue your service with renewed vigour and dedication.*

ABOVE: A late 14th-century manuscript showing archangel Gabriel, artist unknown.

JUSTICE

"A man is a little thing while he works by and for himself;
but when he gives voice to the rules of love and justice, he is godlike."

RALPH WALDO EMERSON (1803–1882)

Justice is judgment tempered by mercy. A vital element in the maintenance of harmony between both individuals and nations, this is something toward which we must all strive. Angels themselves may not judge, but as emissaries of divine justice they ceaselessly battle against evil on our behalf. If you are seeking justice, for yourself or for other people, the angels will support you and stand by you if your cause is righteous and true. While forgiveness is an admirable quality, there are times when justice must become the benchmark of correct action in the world.

TRUTH IN ACTION

✳ *Benjamin Disraeli, the British prime minster, once said that "Justice is truth in action," and this sentiment finds its angelic embodiment in archangel Michael – often depicted with the sword of truth in one hand and the scales of justice in the other. If you seek justice, ask Michael in your prayers or meditations to show you where true justice lies.*

GUARDIANSHIP

"Do not despair, saying, "My life is gone, and the Friend has not come."
He comes ... and out of season. He comes not only at dawn."

RUMI (1207–73)

Each of us has a guardian angel who embodies all the angelic qualities explored in this part of the book. But, most of all, our guardian angels take special care to watch over us, their individual charges, and are available to us as a source of personal inspiration. Some people sense their own angel's presence very clearly, which often happens unexpectedly – perhaps at the borderland between sleeping and waking, or while writing a letter, or walking to the local stores, or commuting to work. For no obvious reason, the appropriate part of the mind becomes attuned to this constant but undemanding, unforceful presence.

Others, however, find that their best contact comes as a result of a specific invocation or meditation. Rest assured: even at times when you cannot feel this presence, your guardian angel is still there, caring for you, loving you. If you had the gift of true insight, you would see his footprints everywhere, running alongside yours.

_____ IN TOUCH WITH YOUR GUARDIAN ANGEL _____

✳ *Develop your own personal formula that acknowledges the unique relationship you have with your guardian angel, and use this as a starting point in communication. You may do this by saying aloud (or to yourself) a prayer, phrase or poem. This needn't be the same one repeatedly — you may like to choose a new text for each day. Or alternatively, you might prefer to open up communication by meditating on a picture or perhaps lighting a candle.*

✳ *Devise a simple method of acknowledging your guardian angel that you are comfortable using in a public place such as a train or the office or even in the movies. One commuter shuts his eyes and reflects on this acronym, based on GUARDIAN ANGEL:"Glory Unto All Regularly Defending Innocence Against Nastiness. And Niceness Gives Enjoyable Life." Eccentric, but it works for him. Something*

similar may work for you.Your guardian angel may never have to save you from a physical accident or a thoughtless decision, but these daily moments of togetherness can bring you spiritual contentment and help you to develop angelic attributes in your life.

✳ *Develop a quality of discreet guardianship in yourself. Just as we are not always aware of the acts of love or protection performed for us by our guardian angels, we can emulate their unseen generosity by cultivating a similar role in the lives of others.Whenever you get the chance, perform an unsolicited act of kindness — such as picking up litter from someone's driveway or pausing to check that a child crosses the street safely. Do this unobserved, expecting no reward other than the pleasure you take in another's happiness or safety.*

ASPIRATION

"Yet some there be that by due steps aspire
To lay their hands on that golden key
That opens the palace of eternity."

JOHN MILTON (1608–74)

Our aspirations ennoble us. Setting our sights on distant goals of self-realization, creative self-expression or selfless service to others, we often think, quite appropriately, in terms of an upward movement – heavenwards. So long as we feel that angels are supporting our worthiest ambitions, we have two reasons to feel good about our prospects: first, because we know that angels are on our side, encouraging us; and second, because we know that every step forward and upward is giving divine pleasure.

KEEP AN ANGEL NOTEBOOK

Whether you have a particular goal (such as completing a course of study) or a general aspiration toward self-development, keeping an angel notebook will help you fulfil it.

1 *Buy yourself a special diary or notebook – ideally, one that is a pleasure to handle. You might like to customize it to make it personal to your angel, or to your goal.*

2 *Before writing a word inside your new notebook, dedicate it to an angel and call on their help as you set out to achieve your ambition. This angel should be one whose attributes you find particularly inspiring, such as Machidiel, who stands for action, creativity and controlled ambition; or Jophiel, whose chief attributes include illumination, inspiration and wisdom.*

3 *Make a note in your notebook of the progress you are making toward achieving your goal, including any angel meditations you have followed and any insights gained from them. Take heart from the support you are receiving from your angel, in helping you through any difficult patches, and guiding you to being a more fulfilled and balanced person.*

ABOVE: *Perugino Angel*, by Tomar Levine (contemporary artist).

HOPE

"Hope is the thing with feathers
That perches in the soul
And sings the tune without the words."

EMILY DICKINSON (1830–86)

Hope is one of the great gifts of the angels. Its great symbol is the dove bearing an olive branch, spied by Noah at the height of the Flood and indicative that the waters had receded. An optimistic outlook on life tends to be self-fulfilling: positive expectations summon positive results. Few days pass when we don't have some reason for expressing a special hope. The angels cannot guarantee the result, but they will help you remain positive, whatever the outcome.

HOPE WITH CONFIDENCE

✳ *Choose a quiet time and place in your day. Put some token of the situation you are concerned about somewhere in your line of vision. Reflect on the Virtues, that mighty angelic order led by Raphael, who transmit a power that can work miracles. Your hope will be transformed into a stronger trust – the confidence that all will come right in the end.*

VISION

"If the eye were not sun-like, it could not see the sun; if we did not carry within us the power of God, how could anything God-like delight us?"

JOHANN WOLFGANG VON GOETHE (1749–1832)

Although they can appear in the material world, angels live elsewhere, in the realm of spirit. As they move between the celestial sphere and our own, one of their most precious gifts to us is the glimpses we can obtain during those brief partings of the curtain – insights into the divine. The angelic perspective is a world away from our own, and gives us much that we can learn from. It is always inspiring – as well as awesome – to see beyond the immediate and the everyday. All of us can tap into the vision of the angels, to help us look beyond the horizon and discern our true path.

THE BIGGER PICTURE

✳ *Imagine yourself as an interdependent element within the cosmos, like the stars. Try to detach yourself from the day-to-day details of your life and view it as the angels might, from above. From this distant perspective, no doubt some of your concerns will seem trivial. But others, related to such eternal qualities as love and faith, will gain new importance.*

ENDURANCE

"We shall find peace. We shall hear the angels,
we shall see the sky sparkling with diamonds."

ANTON CHEKHOV (1860–1904)

We might not imagine that angels, who look upon the face of God, have much to endure. However, we should remember that they are engaged in a perpetual struggle on our behalf with the forces of negation, apathy and malevolence. They are embodiments of the moral strength and courage to which we ourselves aspire. By cultivating endurance in our lives we are making our own important contribution to the angelic cause. And when life feels more about endurance than enjoyment, we can always call on the angels to help us.

In the book of Genesis, Jacob spent a whole night wrestling with an angel, refusing to give in until the being had blessed him as he had been promised by God (GENESIS 32). Afterwards he was given the name "Israel", meaning "He who strives with God". Jacob's story shows us that the rewards of true, sincere, strong behaviour cannot be taken for granted: they must be struggled for. Endurance anneals the soul, attesting to our depth of character, our worthiness for the great rewards of the spirit.

ANGELS IN YOUR CORNER

✴ *If you feel beset by troubles, don't give up — be reassured by the knowledge that the angels are fighting by your side. Ask for help from Adnachiel, for constancy of purpose; Uriel, for strength; or Emmanuel, for protection. Trust that your chosen angel will act appropriately, even if it may not seem like it initially.*

✴ *In a long struggle, each day won, or each day completed with your faith, hope, determination and values intact, is a victory. Offer yourself an incentive (not a self-indulgent one!) to help you face hard times: relax whenever you get the chance in the knowledge that you deserve it.*

ABOVE: *Jacob Fighting the Angel*, 1855–61 fresco (detail), Eugène Delacroix (1798–1863).

COURAGE

"I looked over Jordan and what did I see?
A band of angels comin' after me —
Comin' for to carry me home."

NEGRO SPIRITUAL (*c.*1850)

Courage comes in many forms – it may be seen in the refusal to be defeated by illness or ill-fortune, or in the simple act of saying "no" to somebody who is pressurizing you to do something you know you should not do. The chief angel of courage is the archangelic warrior Michael, whose other attributes include strength and protection. We can all feel inspired by stories of Michael, clad in bright armour, wielding a sword or spear, and fearlessly striking down the dragon of evil. We may not slay dragons any more, but we may feel that our personal demons are legion. The image of Michael triumphant is an encouraging example as we face our life's struggles.

Similarly, the angel Abdiel, in Milton's *Paradise Lost* (1667), is a shining exemplar of moral courage. In the face of great pressure Abdiel refuses to join the rebel angels who surround him, taking a stand against what he knows to be wrong: "Among the faithless, faithful only he." To resist the tide is often the most courageous act of all.

YOUR INVISIBLE WARRIOR

✳ *Whenever you find yourself facing a stressful situation in your life, whether major or minor, call on archangel Michael to stand alongside you and offer you his assistance. Visualize his angelic presence giving you courage, protection and strength.*

ABOVE: *Saint Michael and Other Angels, c.*1373–1410, by Aretino Spinello (*d.*1410).

COMFORT

"Turn to face the sun and the shadows fall behind you."

MAORI PROVERB

In the Christian tradition, even Christ himself was comforted by angels in the Garden of Gethsemane, knowing his arrest and crucifixion to be imminent. Comfort may sound like a luxury, but basic comforts of body, mind and spirit are in fact necessities. However, none of us is wholly immune from the darkness that only divine reassurance can truly dispel – a shadow that may fall from loss, disappointment, failure, betrayal, or any other of fate's many slings and arrows. Divine love, mediated by the angels, is like a fortress: it weathers the fiercest of storms and offers you shelter whenever you need it.

ACCESSING ANGELIC COMFORT

✳ *Look for a beautiful angel picture that you find consoling – perhaps a postcard or an image in this book. Keep it by you, as a reminder of unseen angelic sources of comfort.*

✳ *Perform the meditation on page 92. Use Step 5 to invoke an angelic comforter – perhaps Asmodel (source of dependability and strength) or Manuel (security).*

OPPOSITE: *The Annunciation*, 1638–39 (detail), by Francisco de Zurbarán (1598–1664).

HEALING

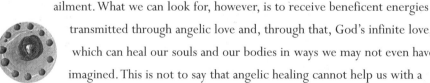

"O God give me strength to be victorious over myself ... O guide my spirit, O raise me from these dark depths, that my soul, transported through Your wisdom, may fearlessly struggle upward in fiery flight. For You alone understand and can inspire me."

LUDWIG VAN BEETHOVEN (1770–1827)

The healing power of angelic love is available to all of us – we just need to make ourselves receptive to it. Archangel Raphael is the great angel of healing, but all angels, as envoys of divine love, can bring a healing presence into our lives. Raphael means "the shining one who heals" – in the apocryphal Book of Tobit, Raphael's work included warding off a troublesome demon and helping to restore Tobit's ailing sight.

If you seek healing, remember that angels are agents of the Divine Will. We cannot simply summon Raphael, or any other angel, and expect a miraculous cure for a specific ailment. What we can look for, however, is to receive beneficent energies transmitted through angelic love and, through that, God's infinite love, which can heal our souls and our bodies in ways we may not even have imagined. This is not to say that angelic healing cannot help us with a physical illness – it may well do this, at least in enabling us to cope with the symptoms. But we should appreciate the depth of spiritual and emotional healing that can be received as well, which in turn may well have physical effects. We can also, of course, ask for angelic assistance in the healing of others, whether these are people we know, or strangers. Wherever there is need, invoke the angels and they will help the whole self.

ANGELIC HEALING

✴ *If you wish to send the healing power of angels to somebody else, visualize the person (or people) concerned. Perhaps write their name on a card, or, if you can, find a photograph of them, and hold this in your hand. Perform the preparatory meditation on p.92, open your heart and mind, and ask Raphael to use you as a channel through which to send a flow of healing energy to the person in need. Remain in the meditative state for as long as you feel is appropriate. Once you have finished, thank Raphael for his help.*

✴ *If you are suffering from an emotional wound that needs to be healed, visualize your pain as a physical wound on your body, and imagine it slowly healing with the help of the loving care you receive from the angels. Ask your own guardian angel, or Raphael, to draw especially near while you are doing this. You may feel that you need only one session to heal your wound, or you may like to perform the exercise repeatedly over a few days. Trust in the healing power of angels, and see if your trust is rewarded – it might well be.*

COMPASSION

"I heard an angel singing
When the day was springing,
'Mercy, pity, peace
Is the world's release.'"

WILLIAM BLAKE (1757–1827)

True compassion flows fast, it has been said — as if we were wounded ourselves, though without diminishing our strength. Loving yourself and letting yourself be loved is the best starting point for showing compassion, in precisely this spirit of resilient empathy. When seeking compassion from an angel, try to avoid both self-pity or self-reproach, both of which cloud the mind. Let the angel through to the very root of your concern. One day you may be able to perform the same service for someone.

THE PATH OF COMPASSION

✳ *Before asking for compassion, for yourself or another, spend a short time looking back over the last year or so and personally acknowledge those times when your own behaviour was less than compassionate. Where you can, address the situation — it is seldom too late to make* amends. Or instead you might choose to ask for forgiveness from the Divine Source. Lifting such burdens from your past will enable you to move forward freely and bring further compassion into your own life and the lives of others.

✳ *If you need to receive compassion into your life as a whole, or into a particular situation, call on the angels Gabriel or Rahmiel, both of whom have mercy as a chief attribute, or Calliel, who brings help in difficult situations.*

✳ *When someone else needs your compassion, quieten your mind (you might like to use the Preparatory Meditation on p.92 to do this) and focus on the person concerned. Ask your guardian angel to act as a divine channel between you and the intended recipient of your compassion, and to direct your boundless love in a stream flowing into their heart.*

LIGHT

"Their garments are white, but with an unearthly whiteness.
These bright Angels are enveloped in a light so different from ours that
by comparison everything else seems dark."

FATHER THEODORE LAMY (1855–1931)

Metaphorically, when we call on the angels for guidance we are asking them to light our way for us. These beings have often been described as shining intensely; and traditionally, of course, their haloes of light are their best-known physical attribute after their wings. By seeking to emulate the angelic qualities inherent in that light, we strive to reflect some of the angels' radiant love into our all too often dark world.

Something of the intensity of angelic light has been glimpsed by those who claim to have experienced a Near Death Experience. One of the most common features of an NDE is the incredibly bright white light to which the person concerned is drawn, often along a tunnel. Our own light, even at its brightest, seems dim beside an angel's.

Light is not only vitalizing, however: it is also revealing. In the illumination of the divine, our natures are guided and purged. When we see our imperfections clearly, they become intolerable to us, and prompt us to take healthy, cleansing action.

A MEDITATION ON ANGEL ENERGY

There is a profound serenity to be drawn from meditating on the flickering, steady flame of a candle: see page 99 for advice on how to approach this. However, an equally effective meditation on the theme of angelic light can be performed inwardly, without any external aids, as described below.

1 Sit comfortably in a quiet place, and close your eyes. Breathe slowly and deeply, so that your body begins to relax a little. Let the tensions fall away from each part of your body in turn, progressing downwards from your head, down your back, and along all four limbs. Try to relax your mind similarly.

2 Identify a mental focus, just in front of your eyes or forehead — wherever seems natural to you. Then imagine the light of an angel's energy beginning to radiate from this point, like a starbirth. Gradually, you imagine the radiance increasing in strength, without the central point of light getting any bigger.

3 Picture the infinite energy that is pouring out from the angel's heart as a flow that enters your own heart, filling you with divine purpose and strength. After a few minutes of recharging your spiritual batteries, see the light fade gradually, its mission accomplished. Your meditation is complete.

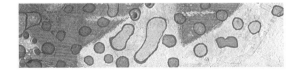

ENJOYMENT

"A song slumbers in all things that lie dreaming on and on and the world prepares to sing, if you hit upon the magic word."

JOSEPH FREIHERR VON EICHENDORFF (1788–1857)

Angels are embodiments of unadulterated joy. In scripture and in art they are often associated with singing and music, and the *putti* of Renaissance paintings have a decidedly playful manner. As bearers of God's love for us, angels want us to be happy, because this is the natural state of the peaceful, virtuous soul. In a world in harmony with itself, and with divine purposes, there is no artificial separation between goodness and pleasure. A life touched by angels will be far from solemn.

TAKE ALONG AN ANGEL

✷ *Angels chiefly associated with the capacity for getting the most out of life are Ambriel, for enthusiasm and participation; and Verchiel, for optimism, gregariousness and helping to ensure that others are enjoying themselves as much as we are. If you are planning an enjoyable event such as a party, Verchiel would be a good companion. For a visit to a gallery, Ambriel will help you to be observant, and rewarded for what you take the trouble to see.*

HOSPITALITY

Do not neglect to show hospitality to strangers, for by doing that
some have entertained angels without knowing it.

Although angels, being visitors themselves, are not usually in a position to show hospitality in the normal sense of the word, they often encourage hospitality in others. In Genesis 18, Abraham received three visitors into his home and gave them the choicest food he had to offer, as he would have done for any unexpected guest. His visitors were in fact angels, and the story serves to underline the message that we should always strive to be generous, even to strangers, and keep an open house and heart. Of course, there is a commonplace utilitarian logic that points to the importance of kindness and hospitality: even at an everyday, practical level, others will treat us as we treat them; an invitee will usually send back a return invite. However, such mundane calculations fall far below angelic standards of goodness. The true path, sanctioned by the divine, is to give freely without hope or even thought of recompense. Every charitable act may be a stepping-stone to heaven, but we give for its own sake, not for our salvation's sake, and from the heart of our loving nature.

THE CIRCLE OF KINDNESS

While it isn't always appropriate or safe to invite complete strangers into your home, you can show them kindness in many practical ways. Perhaps you could volunteer some of your time as a cook in a shelter for the homeless or as a companion in a retirement home.

Cultivate hospitality toward your personal angel. When you meditate and ask an angel to come into your life, treat them as an honoured guest. Prepare a comfortable, attractive space, perhaps with flowers or candles, or even an empty chair for your angelic visitor.

ABOVE: *Still Life of a Table Laden with Food, Drink and a Vase of Flowers*, by Thomas Hiepes (1610–74).

EXCELLENCE

"Everyone should carefully observe which way his heart draws him,
and then choose that way with all his strength."

HASIDIC SAYING

The idea of an angel half-doing something is impossible to imagine. John Milton's *Paradise Lost* (1667) tells of the angels who allowed Satan to slip into the Garden of Eden, "Which your sincerest care," as God points out, "could not prevent". But angels are otherwise completely focused in their actions, with not a hint of reservation, distraction or half-heartedness. What they do, they do excellently. We can all benefit from this angelic example, by refusing to allow muddle or compromise into our thinking, and declining to do less than our best — especially when we are working for other people or in the service of positive values.

BE EXCELLENT

* *Invoke your guardian angel, or an angel particularly endowed with practical skillfulness, such as Casujoiah; or conscientiousness, such as Hamaliel. Ask them to help you to apply their standards of excellence to all aspects of your life, and especially the task in hand. Imagine them watching over you, and guiding your actions.*

* *If you are struggling with an unexciting chore that you are finding unrewarding, try to turn it into an angelic job. Ask for extra encouragement and motivation from the angels. For example, if you are decorating your home, you might enjoy painting the walls, but hate all the initial preparation that is needed. By dedicating every step of the task to your angelic helpers, or to some noble cause, you should get more satisfaction from your work.*

LOVE

"Love possesses seven hundred wings,
and each one extends from the highest heaven
to the lowest earth."

RUMI (1207–73)

Love is the underlying message of all the angels, the great divine subtext. Essentially, angels embody the love of the Creator for His creation, and in a harmonious world all this love is reflected back toward its Source by all created beings. It transcends all limitations and is beyond our powers of description. Although it may be difficult for us to grasp its infinite scope and purity, the truth is that we too are capable of transmitting our own love to the living world, including everyone we meet, in endless abundance. God has supplied us with capacities that soar beyond the limits of the physical.

LOVE IN ACTION

✳ *Start by practising loving care toward your family and close friends, before moving on to acquaintances. Even simple gestures, such as giving flowers or tidying a room, are aptly symbolic of our love. Invoke Hamaliel, angel of family life, to inspire you in this.*

✴ *Similarly, offer loving care to the environment, by recycling, reducing waste, driving less, or simply picking up litter. Ask the help of the angel Carviel, high among the Principalities, who helps to maintain order and structure in creation.*

✴ *Remember to offer loving thoughts to your guardian angel regularly. Angelic love is given without expectation, and your own love should be offered in the same way — even though there is always a karmic benefit that will help to make you happier.*

✴ *You'll find it easy to give love to people you already love. Try also to cultivate love for someone about whom you care little, or even dislike. Loving our enemies can have the most powerful and transforming effect imaginable on both the giver and the receiver of the love.*

MUSIC

And let the base of heaven's deep organ blow,
And with your ninefold harmony
Make up the full consort to the angelic symphony.

JOHN MILTON (1608–74)

Angels have always been associated with beautiful music. The Greeks spoke of the music of the heavenly spheres, and angelic choirs and musicians have been depicted in art for centuries. Fine music is a pleasure of the heart, even a kind of inward conversation with the divine. The "Gloria", part of the Mass, conjures up the praise to God sung by the angels who appeared to shepherds on the morning of Christ's nativity. Angels with particular musical associations are Israfel, Shamiel and the Bene Elim.

MOOD MUSIC

* When seeking an angelic visitation, try using music to help you attune to an angel's wavelength. Listen to something quiet and contemplative, such as plainsong. Some people find a natural sound is best, such as recorded bird-song, or the slow, deep music of whales.

OPPOSITE: *The Angel with the Trumpet*, c.1884, by Herbert Horne (1864–1916).

HARMONY

"Two things fill the mind with ever new and increasing admiration and awe, the oftener and more steadily we reflect on them: the starry heavens above and the moral law within."

IMMANUEL KANT (1724–1804)

Humankind has a habit of separating itself from God, and one of the roles of the angels is to repair the breach and restore harmony to the cosmos. Sandalphon, the giant angel of Gnostic tradition, whose feet are at the roots of the Tree of Knowledge and who rises high into the stars to support the heavenly firmament, is a guiding principle of this universal order. The Qur'an speaks of angels who "sing the praise of the Lord and ask for forgiveness for those on earth" – a two-way transaction that binds and balances the universe in a perfect symmetry and establishes a true relationship between humankind and the divine. Just as harmony is the ideal condition of the cosmos, so too it is sought in all our relations with God, our fellow human beings and all living things. This does not mean that hierarchies in themselves are a positive good – we all know that over-punctilious distinctions of rank can cause unrest in a social group. But there is a natural order – and loving, selfless relationships are the threads that keep it together.

— SPREAD ANGELIC HARMONY —

✳ *Don't despair of the endless conflicts and seeming lack of effective mediation in the wider world. Instead, focus on bringing a little harmony to a situation closer to home. Take the next available opportunity to mediate between friends, family members or co-workers who are at odds with each other. However small your contribution, it will be a positive one and will aid the angels in their bid to bring harmony to the world as a whole. If you are unsure or nervous about offering to help, ask a mediating angel, such as Rahmiel, an agent of benevolence and mercy, to give you confidence and conviction in your actions. Efforts of this kind are often more than a drop in the ocean: they can change the ocean currents in a meaningful way.*

PRAISE

"And you shall see the angels going round about the throne glorifying the praise of their Lord; and judgment shall be given between them with justice, and it shall be said: All praise is due to Allah."

THE QUR'AN

Cynical minds have often mocked the concept of the angels' perpetual chorus of praise and the Almighty's supposed appetite for it. But that is perhaps because, on the earthly plane, praise is often debased into flattery and self-image often has a perpetual hunger for reassurance. Not so at the divine level. Imitate the angels by praising only when you are sincere, and be unstinting in your praise.

PRACTISE PRAISING

* *Encourage a positive attitude in the world around you by always looking for the best in people, in events, and in your own life. Pay somebody a sincere compliment today, and watch their self-esteem increase. Praise yourself, too, especially when you achieve something nobody else notices. Make the showing of due appreciation a daily task.*

OPPOSITE: *The Assumption of the Virgin Mary* (detail), by Girolamo di Benvenuto (1470–1524).

GLOSSARY OF ANGELS

This guide is designed to help you learn more about individual angels and their particular attributes. You may wish to call upon them by name or ask for their help as you work at developing certain angelic qualities in your life.

Only four angels are named in the Bible, and of these two are Fallen Angels. The names of the other angels in this guide come from a range of ancient and modern sources. This list gives the most generally accepted names, but is by no means exhaustive. Its main source is the non-canonical Book of Enoch, but some names from the Gnostic tradition are included.

Some of the associations attributed to particular angels – with zodiac signs, for example – can vary widely from source to source, and derive largely from contemporary New Age thought. Again, this guide presents the most commonly accepted associations.

Remember that it is not necessary to know an angel's name in order to feel an angel's presence. It may be that in your own angelic encounters your guardian angel will reveal his name to you.

Why do so many of the names end in -iel? Because the Hebrew word for God is El, and most of the Hebrew angel names refer to an aspect or attribute of God, as with Gabriel, "God is my Strength".

ABDIEL: Servant of God. Found in the Kabbalistic Book of the Angel Raziel. This angel, at first tempted to join Satan, remains with the angels loyal to God in Milton's *Paradise Lost* (1650–60). The name comes from the Book of Chronicles in the Bible (as a man's name).

ADNACHIEL: Ruler of the month of November; also angel of the star-sign Sagittarius.

ADONAI: One of the seven Angels of the Presence, who look upon the face of God. In the Old Testament, Adonai is used as a name for God.

AIEL: Angel of the star-sign Aries and the month of March. Also known as Machidiel.

AMBRIEL: An angel of the Order of Thrones. Angel of the star-sign Gemini and of the month of May.

ANAEL: One of the seven Angels of Creation. Holds dominion over the planet Venus, and so over human sexuality.

ANGEL OF DEATH: Michael, in the Christian tradition; Azrael, in the Islamic tradition.

ANGELS: According to the Dionysian scheme, Angels themselves form a specific Order within the overall hierarchy: the Ninth and lowest Order, though still vastly higher than post-Fall humanity. This is the Order most directly in contact with mortals. Prince of this Order is Gabriel.

ARCHANGELS: In the Dionysian scheme, they form the Eighth Order, as heralds and agents of revelation, with Michael as their prince. The non-Biblical Book of Enoch notes also Uriel, Raguel, Sariel and Jerahmeel as Archangels. In the Christian tradition Michael's role far transcends that of Prince of the Eighth Order, and Archangels are thought of as the leaders of the entire angelic host.

ASMODEL: Angel of the star-sign Taurus and the month of April.

AUSIEL: Angel of the star-sign Aquarius and the month of January.

AZARIAS: The name by which Raphael made himself known to Tobit.

AZRAEL: Whom God helps. The Angel of Death. In Christian angel-lore this has become one of the titles of Michael.

BARADIEL: One of the seven great Archangels of the Book of Enoch.

BARAKIEL: Also written Barchiel. One of the seven great Archangels; Angel with dominion over lightning. Also the angel of the star-sign Pisces and the month of February.

BARUCH: Chief angel of the Tree of Life. The same name is also used of a demon, one of the devils who troubled the nuns of Loudoun, in France.

BENE ELIM: The angels who ceaselessly sing the praises of God.

CARVIEL: High among the order of Principalities, and an angel who helps maintain order and structure in creation.

CALLIEL: A Throne, invoked for help in adversity.

CAMAEL: "He who sees God". Prince of the Order of Powers.

CASSIEL: One of the Powers, the angel of solitude and tears.

CASUJOIAH: Angel of the star-sign Capricorn and the month of December.

CHALKYDRI: The twelve-winged angels of the Sun, who sing to greet its rising.

CHARBIEL: The angel sent to end the Flood.

CHERUBIM: The name, from an Assyrian origin, means one who prays or intercedes. Also known as The Shining Ones. The first angels mentioned in the Hebrew Bible, guardians of the Tree of Life and the Garden of Eden. Prior to the Fall, Satan was their chief. In the Dionysian scheme, Cherubim were the Second Order, angels of light and keepers of records. Their prince is Ophaniel.

DARK ANGEL: The angel who wrestled with Jacob – unnamed but identified variously as Peniel, Metatron, Michael or Uriel.

DOMINIONS: The Fourth Order in the Dionysian scheme. The marshals of the angelic host. Zadkiel is prince of this order.

ELOHIM: A generic word for the angels. It is also a synonym for Yahweh, and in the Hebrew Bible may mean God, the angels, or both together.

EMMANUEL: The angel who protected Shadrach, Meshach and Abednego in the fiery furnace (see Daniel 3.1–29).

FOUR ARCHANGELS: These are given in the Book of Enoch as Michael, Gabriel, Raphael and Phanuel. In other sources Uriel replaces Phanuel.

GABRIEL: "God is my Strength". The Archangel of the Annunciation, and of resurrection, mercy, vengeance, revelation and death. One of the very few angels mentioned by name in the Bible. Prince of the Order of Angels. It was Gabriel who inspired Joan of Arc in her fight to restore the kingdom of France. He is said to have left a footprint in stone at New Harmony, Indiana, on a visit to the Harmonite community founded by George Rapp in 1805. An alternative to Ausiel as angel of the star-sign Aquarius and the month of January.

GAMALIEL: The reward of God. One of the angels who draws the chosen up to heaven.

GRAIL ANGELS: The angels who protect the Holy Grail in Arthurian legend. "Then looked he up in the midst of the chamber, and saw a table of silver, and the holy vessel, covered with red samite, and many angels about it" (*Le Morte d'Arthur* (1485) by Sir Thomas Mallory).

HADRANIEL: Majesty of God. A keeper of the heavenly gates. "When Hadraniel proclaims the will of the Lord, his voice penetrates through twenty thousand firmaments" (Zoharic legend).

HAHAIAH: One of the Cherubim, who influences the thoughts of mortals, and reveals mysteries.

HAMALIEL: Ruler of the star-sign Virgo and the month of August.

HANIEL: Also written Hanael. "He who sees God". Chief of the Principalities. An alternative to Casujoiah as angel of the star-sign Capricorn and the month of December.

HAZIEL: One of the Cherubim, invoked in order to obtain the pity of God.

HERALD ANGEL: Raziel.

ISRAEL: An angel of the Order of Thrones.

ISRAFEL: Also written Israfil. In Islam, the angel who will blow the trumpet on the Last Day. He preceded Gabriel as the spiritual guide and companion to the Prophet. The Qur'an says: "Israfel, whose heartstrings are a lute, and who has the sweetest voice of all God's creatures."

ITHURIEL: Discovery of God. An angel of the Order of Principalities. It was Ithuriel (in *Paradise Lost*) whose spear touched Satan in the Garden of Eden, disguised as a toad, and made him take his own shape.

JOPHIEL: One of the order of Cherubim. An angel of knowledge, wisdom, insight and creativity, and patron of artists. In Jewish tradition, Jophiel is a companion to the archangel Metatron.

JOEL: A name of Metatron, who had many names. One of the angels who conversed with Adam.

LAMACH: Ruler of the planet Mars.

MACHIDIEL: "Fullness of God". Angel of the star-sign Aries and the month of March.

MALIK: The Islamic angel in charge of Hell.

MANUEL: Bringer of comfort and security.

MAYMON: Chief angel of the air.

MELCHISEDEK: One of the Order of Virtues. An agent of divine grace.

METATRON: This name is not in the Bible-record, but Gnostic writings make him greatest of all the angels, chief of the Seraphim, seen as a vital link between the human and the divine. He was seen as the pillar of smoke and fire that led the Israelites through the desert. The source of the name is obscure, probably deliberately so. Meta- as a Greek prefix means "changing". Jewish tradition believes that Metatron is the prophet Enoch transformed. Metatron was often referred to by other names, referring to specific aspects of his splendour and power.

MICHAEL: "Who is as God". The supreme Archangel in the Christian tradition. His name comes from that of a Chaldean divinity. He is prince of the Order of Archangels, and angel of repentance, righteousness, mercy and courage. He led the loyal angels and is often depicted as armoured, striking down Satan in the form of a dragon or serpent. He is also sometimes shown with the scales of justice, symbolic of his role on Judgement Day. In the 20th century, Michael was named as patron saint of law enforcement by the Catholic Church.

MORONI: The angel seen on numerous occasions in the 1820s, by Joseph Smith at Hill Cumorah, New York. Here Smith received "the gospel of a new revelation", the basis of Mormonism.

MURIEL: Bringer of myrrh. The angel of June and of the star-sign Cancer.

NINE ORDERS AND THEIR PRINCES: *The First Hierarchy*: The Seraphim (Metatron), The Cherubim (Ophaniel), The Thrones (Zaphkiel). *The Second Hierarchy*: The Dominions (Zadkiel), The Virtues (Raphael), The Powers (Camael). *The Third Hierarchy*: The Principalities (Haniel), The Archangels (Michael), the Angels (Gabriel). The original prince of the Cherubim was Samael (Satan).

NISROC: The name comes from that of an Assyrian deity but Milton in *Paradise Lost* (1650–60) makes him a chief of the Order of Principalities. In occult lore he is a demon.

OPHANIEL: The derivation of the name is linked to Thrones and Wheels. The chief of the Order of Thrones, in some sources, with dominion over the Moon, but more generally regarded as the chief of the Order of Cherubim.

ORIFIEL: A Throne. One of a number of angels with dominion over Saturn.

PASIEL: Alternative to Barakiel as angel of the star-sign Pisces and the month of February.

PENIEL: Face of God. Identified as the angel who wrestled with Jacob, though other angels have also been suggested.

PHALEC: Also written Phaleg. Chief of the Order of Angels (a role also assigned to Gabriel), with dominion over the planet Mars.

PHANUEL: One of the seven Archangels of the Book of Enoch.

POWERS: The Sixth Order of Angels, whose charge is to counteract the doings of evil spirits. Their prince is Camael.

PRINCIPALITIES: The Seventh Order of Angels, with command over the Eighth and Ninth Orders. Their prince is Haniel, and they have responsibility for maintaining the universal order.

PSYCHOPOMP: An angel with the charge of escorting souls: traditionally a function of Sandalphon or Michael.

RADUERIEL: The Recording Angel; the angel of poetry.

RAGUEL: Friend of God. One of the seven great Archangels of the Book of Enoch.

RAHMIEL: Also written Rachmiel. An angel of mercy.

RAMIEL: One of the seven Archangels of the Book of Enoch. An angel of vengeance, in the Vision of Baruch he destroyed Sennacherib's army. A Fallen Angel in Milton's *Paradise Lost* (1650–60).

RAPHAEL: One of the named Biblical angels, Raphael is the angel recorded in the Book of Tobit as having escorted the youth Tobias in Egypt. He makes himself known as "One of the seven, who stand before the Lord." The name means "God has Healed", and he is the angel of healing; also of the Sun, prayer, joy, love and light. He is Chief of the Order of Virtues.

RAZIEL: Secret of God. The master of holy wisdom. The occult medieval Book of the Angel Raziel was supposedly written by him.

RECORDING ANGEL: Radueriel. Also often given as Metatron.

RIDWAN: The Islamic angel who presides over the angels of heaven.

SACHIEL: One of the Cherubim, with charge over the planet Jupiter.

SANDALPHON: In Kabbalistic lore, one of the greatest angels, twin brother of Metatron.

SERAPHIM: The First Order of Angels, who stand before God and behold his face. The name in

Hebrew means "flaming ones". Their prince, in the Judaic tradition, is Metatron.

SEVEN ARCHANGELS: The seven great Archangels listed in the Book of Enoch are Uriel, Raphael, Michael, Sariel, Gabriel, Remiel, Raguel. Other sources list other names.

SHAMIEL: The master of heavenly song.

SURIEL: A name also identified with Uriel and Metatron; angel of healing and also of death.

THRONES: The Third Order of Angels, the "god-bearers". Their prince is Zaphkiel.

TSADKIEL: Angel of justice, in the Kabbalistic lists.

URIEL: Fire of God. A great angel, denoted both as one of the Seraphim and the Cherubim. In Milton's *Paradise Lost* (1650–60), he stood at the gate of Eden with a flaming sword.

URIZEN: Identified by William Blake as the Angel of England, in *The Book of Urizen*.

UZZIEL: In some lists ranked as Chief of the Virtues.

VERCHIEL: Angel of the star-sign Leo, and of the month of July.

VIRTUES: The fifth Order of Angels. Filled with divine strength, they transmit the power to work miracles. Their prince is Raphael.

WHEELS: In some sources, an Order of Angels, most approximate to the Thrones. They are depicted as winged wheels, with many eyes.

ZACHARAEL: Remembrance of God.

ZADKIEL: Righteousness of God. Angel of benevolence, mercy, memory. Chief of the Order of Dominions.

ZAPHIEL: Angel who rules over Saturn.

ZAPHKIEL: Chief of the Order of Thrones.

ZEPHON: One of the Cherubim. In *Paradise Lost*, he hunts for Satan with Ithuriel.

ZURIEL: God is my Rock. Prince of the Principalities; also angel of the star-sign Libra.

BIBLIOGRAPHY

Aquinas, St Thomas, *Summa Theologiae* Volume 9
(ia. 50–64): Angels, (ed. and trans. Kenelm
Foster) London: Blackfriars/Eyre &
Spottiswoode; New York: McGraw Hill (1968)

Astell, Christine, *Discovering Angels*, London:
Duncan Baird Publishers (2005)

Carey, Jacqueline, *Angels: Celestial Spirits in Legend
and Art*, New York: Metro Books (1997)

Cohn, Norman, *Cosmos, Chaos & the World to Come*,
London: Yale University Press (1995)

Connelly, Douglas, *Angels Around Us*, Illinois:
Intervarsity Press (1994)

Cooper, Diana, *Angel Inspiration*, London:
Hodder and Stoughton (2001)

Cortens, Theolyn, *Living with Angels*, London:
Piatkus Books (2003)
—, *The Angel's Script*, Oxford: Caer Sidi
Publications (1997)

Dadi Janki, *Wings of Soul*, London: Brahma
Kumaris (1998)

Daniel, Alma, Timothy Wyllie, and Andrew
Ramer, *Ask your Angels*, Canada: Ballantine
Books (1992); London: Piatkus Books (1995)

Davidson, Gustav, *A Dictionary of Angels*, New
York: Simon & Schuster (1967)

Fox, Leonard, and Donald L. Rose, eds.,
*Conversations with Angels: What Swedenborg
Heard in Heaven* (David Gladish and
Jonothan Rose trans.), London: Chrysalis
Books (1996)

Godwin, Malcolm, *Angels: an Endangered Species*,
New York: Simon & Schuster (1990)

Graham, Billy, *Angels: God's Secret Agents*, London:
Hodder & Stoughton (1986)

Guiley, Rosemary Ellen, *Ask the Angels,* London:
Element Books (2003)

Heathcote-James, Emma, *Seeing Angels*, London: John Blake Publishing (2001)

Hodson, Geoffrey, *The Kingdom of Gods*, London: Theosophical Publishing (1976)
——, *The Brotherhood of Angels and of Men*, London: Theosophical Publishing (1927)

McIntosh, J. ed., *Angels, a Joyous Celebration*, Philadelphia: Courage Books (1996)

Moolenburgh, H.C., *Meetings with Angels*, Essex: C. W. Daniel Co (1992)
——, *A Handbook of Angels*, Essex: C. W. Daniel Co (1993)

Neylon, Margaret, *An Angel a Day*, London: Element Books (2003)
——, *Angel Magic*, London: Element Books (2001)

Pearson, Gena, ed., *Cherubs, a Joyous Celebration*, Philadelphia: Courage Books (1998)

Porter, J.R., *The Lost Bible,* London: Duncan Baird Publishers (2001)

Price, Hope, *Angels*, London: Macmillan (1993)

Price, John Randolph, *The Angels Within Us*, London: Piatkus Books (1993)

Printz, Thomas, *The Mighty Elohim Speak*, California: Bridge to Freedom, (1957)
——, *The Seven Beloved Archangels Speak*, California: Ascended Master Teaching Foundation (1954)

Prophet, Elizabeth Clare, *How to Work with Angels*, Montana: Summit University Press (1998)

Serres, Michel, *Angels: A Modern Myth*, France: Flammarion (1993)

Taylor, Richard, *How to Read a Church*, London: Rider Books (2003)

Virtue, Doreen, *Healing with the Angels*, California and London: Hay House Inc. (2001)

Wauters, Ambika, *The Angel Oracle: Working with the Angels for Guidance, Inspiration and Love*, London: Connections Book Publishing (1996)
——, *The Angelic Year*, London: Carroll & Brown (2000)

White, Ruth, *Working with Guides and Angels*, London: Piatkus Books (1996)

INDEX

PICTURE CREDITS

AA The Art Archive, London
BAL The Bridgeman Art Library, London
BM Copyright The Trustees of The British Museum, London